LOST TREASURES

OF AMERICAN HISTORY

W. C. JAMESON

MJF BOOKS • NEW YORK

Published by MJF Books
Fine Communications
322 Eighth Avenue
New York, NY 10001

Lost Treasures of American History
LC Control Number: 2009940531
ISBN-13: 978-1-60671-006-7
ISBN-10: 1-60671-006-0

WCM   10   9   8   7   6   5   4   3   2   1

CONTENTS

LOST
TREASURES
OF AMERICAN
HISTORY

INTRODUCTION

Notes from a Treasure Hunter

I've been a professional fortune hunter for nearly half a century. I've experienced a number of successes and a great many failures searching for lost mines and buried treasure. Regardless of whether or not a treasure was located, the quest was invariably rewarding and fulfilling, and after many years I realized that it was not so much the treasure that lured us, but the quest itself.

Of all of the experiences and adventures I've encountered during my lifetime, few compare to the thrill and excitement associated with the search for, and, if lucky, the discovery of some famous lost mine or elusive buried treasure. I've earned my living in a variety of ways over the years as a professional fighter, dock worker, lifeguard, musician, college professor, writer, and actor, but none ever offered the excitement and adventure of the hunt for lost treasure.

To my way of thinking, there are many good reasons for being a treasure hunter. My work takes me into the great outdoors, to the mountain ranges of the Rockies, Ozarks, and Appalachians, to the shores of the Gulf of Mexico, the Caribbean, and the Atlantic Ocean, to the deserts of the Southwest, the canyons and forests of Mexico's Sierra Madres, and to the island of Jamaica. I've had jobs where I was scheduled to work in an office all day, but found them stifling and constrictive. These days, my office is the world, and I look forward to going to work every day.

As a professional treasure hunter I am constantly in the position of exploring and discovering. I get to visit places mapped and unmapped—mountain ranges, caverns, remote valleys—and revel in the sensation that few, if any, have been in these places before me. When I relate my experiences about such remote and unknown locations, my office- and classroom-bound friends often express terror at such things, unable to imagine a life away from cell phones and televisions. The ritual and regimentation of the nine-to-five job in the same place every working day suits them just fine. Some people are built for such mundane things and I'm pleased we have them to pursue whatever necessary responsibilities they have. I do not possess the qualifications for such work because I am too accustomed, too addicted, to the adrenaline rush of exploration, discovery, and adventure, and cannot, will not, settle for less.

I regard a day without some kind of adventure as a day wasted. A day where the senses go unstimulated or unchallenged is a day pulling one closer to the grave. It is a portion of a life deprived of important sensations. Except for occasionally being shot at, pursued by bandits, falling off cliffs, evading rattlesnake strikes, and crawling through dangerous caves and mine shafts, I am convinced my lifestyle is a healthier way of living. I may not live as long as some of my friends who lead much safer lives as accountants, teachers, and businessmen, and who consider their sedentary lifestyle a sign of success, but the quality of the life and living I rub shoulders with each day cannot be topped for one who revels in the pursuit of adventure.

Finally, there is the prospect of finding wealth. I have been involved in over two hundred major treasure hunting expeditions and dozens of minor ones. Not every expedition ends with some amazing discovery. A number of my expeditions were successful in terms of finding a treasure, but many were not. On the other hand, even though the goal of locating some lost mine or buried loot may not have been achieved, each expedition was filled with adventure and excitement, which is a kind of special treasure in itself.

During some of the talks I give on treasure hunting around the country, people often ask where I find information and leads pertinent to undertaking a search for some lost or buried treasure. Most of the initial information I find, most of the leads I encounter related to chasing down a lost treasure, are gleaned from researching the legend, the lore, and the written history. I spend hours each month in libraries, among private collections of books, journals, and diaries, and interviewing other treasure hunters.

Some of the most exciting and exhilarating searches have resulted from reading and researching American history that deals with the times of the earliest visits to this hemisphere by the Spanish explorers and conquistadores to the present. Recorded history is rich with clues to lost fortunes, hundreds of them. Additionally, studying the history of the Americas, particularly the United States, fills one with wonder and awe at the many heroes encountered, the obstacles they had to face to accomplish what they did, and the seemingly insurmountable odds confronting the early explorers, traders, settlers, and adventurers. History is itself a great treasure, and if pursued with passion, can lead to any number of great adventures.

Ultimately, in my line of work it becomes not only a quest for the treasure, but for the history as well. In understanding the recorded events surrounding a certain treasure, whether it be some gangster's buried loot, a pirate stash, hidden coins from a train or bank robbery, or the caching of hundreds of gold ingots from a Spanish pack train, one will be better prepared to undertake the search, the quest, after one undertakes a thorough examination of the historical events surrounding it. Remember, ninety percent of the research and work associated with any given treasure hunting project takes place not in the field, but in libraries. Maybe one will experience success at finding a treasure, maybe not, but one will certainly come away better versed in some segment of history or another. For me, the challenge of learning about the various aspects of American history has been rewarding, enlightening, and helpful to my searches. Furthermore, it has been fun.

Lost Treasures of American History contains some of the most compelling tales of lost mines and buried treasures I've ever experienced. Here, the reader can learn about fortunes great and small associated with the Spanish occupation of the New World, particularly in the western part of the country. Much of our heritage, culture, and history was formed during the times of the Spanish exploration of the American West, the establishment of missions, the settling of what have come to be major cities and regions, and the early establishment of farming, ranching, and mining enterprises. The Spanish, as much or more than anyone else, were important contributors to this country's collection of legend and lore as it relates to lost mines and buried treasures.

Likewise, the colonial period of North America gave rise to a number of fascinating events resulting in lost treasure that is still being searched for today. During this time, wars were fought for the rights and freedom of the new citizens occupying the land, ultimately giving rise to national leaders such as George Washington and other major historic figures like Benedict Arnold and Edward Braddock. This time in the development of the country also gave rise to numerous tales of lost and stolen treasures.

During the Civil War, money, gold and silver, lots of it, was required by both Union and Confederate armies to sustain their efforts. Millions of dollars worth of gold and silver coins and ingots were lost, misplaced, stolen, or hidden during this time, and today most of it remains un-claimed.

Lastly, some of American history's most recognizable and colorful figures have been outlaws, and many of them have been associated with stolen loot that has been lost or hidden and continues to be the object of many a treasure hunter's quest for fortune. In the last section of the book, we learn about treasures hidden by famous outlaws such as Belle Starr, Sam Bass, and Henry Plummer, and some lesser known bad men like Tiburcio Vasquez and Black Jack Christian. All made their contribution to this collection of tales.

With each of these stories I have a personal investment of time, en-ergy, and money associated with the quest, with the search for the wealth and riches described herein. All of them continue to offer a lure, a chal-lenge, and they are still on my list of objectives for the future. My list is a long one, and I am currently occupied with several projects that may take years. In the meantime, I present them to you for your enjoyment. And if you are so inclined, perhaps you may find yourself undertaking a search for one or more of the treasures described here. Like others who have pursued lost treasure based on descriptions from my books, I wish you the best of good fortune and pray for your success. May you find riches beyond your wildest dreams. But most of all, may you encounter the adventure of a lifetime.

I

SPANISH EXPLORATION AND SETTLEMENT

LOST SPANISH TREASURE SHIP
IN THE CALIFORNIA DESERT

In Southern California, a vast, arid region extends from the present channel of the Colorado River at the Arizona boundary westward for one hundred miles and south across the Mexican border. It is called the Colorado Desert and is largely avoided by humans, animals, and vegetation alike. The constantly blowing winds, the extremely high temperatures, the paucity of water, and the ever-shifting sands have historically precluded any significant permanent occupation. Save for an occasional rattlesnake, scorpion, buzzard, or squatter, most of this land is uninhabited and unvisited. Only the most adventurous or savage, the hopelessly lost, or the eternally optimistic prospectors and miners in search of precious metals in exposed granite outcrops wander here.

This spare and sere desert that straddles the national boundary between California and the Mexican state of Baja California Norte has been described as dangerous and forbidding, and hikers and explorers regularly succumb to its heady challenges and lose their lives as a result of dehydration, exposure, or rattlesnake bite.

This harsh land also carries with it an aura of mystery, and one of its most puzzling secrets is that of a centuries-old, treasure-laden Spanish ship believed to be resting among the ever-shifting dunes somewhere near the middle of this treacherous landscape.

During the mid- to late 1800s, thousands of migrants from east of the Mississippi River packed up and traveled west to California. Some journeyed to the gold fields of California and other western states hoping to strike it rich. Others yearning for land and a place to settle and raise their families found opportunities in the fertile river valleys of California. Many of the migrants passed through this barren, treeless, and waterless wasteland in the southern part of the state. Hundreds died along the way, and every now and then the grave of one can be found among the dunes. Most, however, survived, and not a few arrived on the coast with reports of seeing a masted sailing vessel partially buried in the shining sands. It has been told that some, lured by the possibilities of what they might find within the landlocked ship, returned to the area in search of it only to become lost. Anyone fortunate enough to find the ship would have been rewarded with wealth suitable for a thousand kings, for over 250 years earlier, this same vessel was transporting untold millions of dollars worth of exquisite pearls, all stored in large wooden casks strapped down in the hold.

The story of the lost treasure of pearls in the desert of southern California had its origins four centuries ago. In 1610, Philip III, the reigning king of Spain, ordered Captain Alvarez de Cordone to arrange for an expedition along the waters of the western coast of Mexico in search of pearls. Cordone, stationed in Mexico City, was a well-respected officer and known for his staunch loyalty to the crown. King Philip was eager to fill his country's treasury with some of the great wealth he was certain could be found just off the western shores of this land across the sea. During this time, pearls were considered to be more valuable than gold or silver and were coveted by the Spanish upper class as well as by other members of European royalty.

According to his instructions, Cordone was to oversee the construction of three ships and see to their proper and precise outfitting for the coming expedition. Cordone requested the reassignment of two additional captains, Juan de Iturbe and Pedro de Rosales, and together the three men, accompanied by an armed escort, traveled 250 miles south to the western coastal village of Acapulco. While the three captains supervised the building of the vessels, Cordone was granted the authority to import sixty experienced pearl divers from the east coast of Africa.

In July 1612, the three ships were finally completed, tested for seaworthiness, and declared ready. Cordone led the expedition into the waters of the Pacific Ocean and along a northwesterly course paralleling the Mexico shore.

It was well known among Spanish explorers that the western shore of Mexico was home to a rare large mollusk that produced an exceptional pearl, one that had a dark, shiny, metallic surface. These pearls were prized by wealthy Europeans, and King Philip hoped to be able to supply enough to those who had the money to pay for them.

As the three ships slowly made their way through the placid coastal waters, occasional stops were ordered so the divers could examine and harvest promising oyster beds encountered along the way. While some pearls were found, Cordone knew that the richest beds lay farther north and deeper into the Gulf of California. It was to this area he directed his ships.

Following a few leisurely weeks of sailing, the Spaniards spied a large Indian village near the shore and noted that some of the men appeared to be diving for pearls in the shallow waters. Suspecting he might locate some prize specimens among those accumulated by the Indians, Cordone ordered the anchors dropped. After lowering one of the rowboats, the captain, escorted by a contingent of soldiers and crewmen, put ashore to speak with the village chief.

The Spaniards were the first Europeans the Indians had ever seen. Although Cordone anticipated a hostile reception, he and his men were greeted warmly and invited to share an evening meal. Employing signs and gestures, Cordone and the chief communicated well into the night and much of the next day. Eventually, the captain approached the subject of the pearls being harvested from the sea floor. The chief explained that the oysters were collected primarily for food, but when they found a pearl inside, they stored it with others that were saved for those among the tribe who fashioned necklaces, earrings, and other types of ornamentation from them. When the captain asked if he could see the pearls, the chief obliged. Cordone was surprised and delighted to be shown over two dozen large clay pots filled to the top with the finest stones he had ever seen.

Cordone asked the chief if he would like to trade for the pearls, and offered some clothes such as those worn by the soldiers and sailors. Impressed by the raiment worn by the officers, the chief readily agreed and anticipated garbing himself and some of his tribe in such finery as possessed by these newcomers. Following several minutes of negotiation, an agreement was made and Cordone, along with his escort, returned to the vessel.

The next morning, several neatly tied bundles of clothing were deposited on the shore in exchange for the pots filled with pearls. After the precious stones were placed into rowboats and transported back to the ships, the Indians opened the bundles only to discover a motley collection of rags and discarded garments. They screamed invectives at the departing Spaniards and made angry gestures. Some of the men waded far out into the waters and shot arrows toward the ships. Others piled into log canoes and rowed toward the ships, brandishing bows and arrows and lances.

After loading the pearls into the ship commanded by Iturbe, Cordone ordered the sails hoisted and the vessels under way. As he stood at the rails and watched the angry Indians approaching in canoes, an arrow struck him in the chest, dropping him to the deck. As the ships moved away from the shore, the expedition's surgeon fussed over Cordone's serious wound.

The following morning, Cordone was suffering great pain from his wound and had a high fever. The surgeon was convinced the captain had blood poisoning, and he told Cordone it was imperative to return to Acapulco where he could be more adequately treated. Otherwise, insisted the surgeon, the captain would die.

Cordone agreed with the diagnosis and instructed Iturbe and Rosales to continue on up the coast and into the Gulf of California with the other two ships and harvest more pearls. Once in the far reaches of the gulf, he explained, they would be close to a major breeding ground for the pearl-bearing oysters.

A few weeks later, the two ships captained by Iturbe and Rosales arrived in the Gulf of California. As Cordone had predicted, they discovered several rich mollusk beds that yielded great quantities of the dark, gleaming pearls. As the divers harvested the wealth from the floor of the sea, the two captains determined to sail as far north as possible in hope of finding more and larger oyster beds. They believed that if they returned to Acapulco with the ships loaded with a great cargo of pearls they would be rewarded with promotions and important assignments. This ever-growing desire for power and military status was to prove their undoing.

Iturbe was convinced that the richest oyster beds were to be found where the upper part of the gulf constricts near the outflow of the Colorado River, and it was to this location they steered. The ship under the command of Captain Rosales was struggling because it was riding very low in the water from its great weight of pearls. One afternoon as the vessel was gliding northward in the calm waters just off the coast of an island, Isla Angel de Guardia, it struck a reef which tore a large hole in the oaken hull. As the ship slowly settled into the blue waters of the sea, the crewmen worked frantically transferring the cargo of pearls onto the remaining vessel. This done, the lone ship with a cargo hold almost completely filled with casks of pearls now floated dangerously low in the sea. In spite of this, Captains Iturbe and Rosales decided to continue sailing northward in search of more oyster beds and, they hoped, greater wealth for the Spanish crown.

Two weeks later, Iturbe's ship sailed into the turbid estuarine waters where the Colorado River entered the Gulf of California. During this time, the river carried a much greater flow than it does today. Approximately sixty miles upstream, the river had spilled out of its channel into a basin-like lowland that extended many miles to the west of the main channel, forming a large inland sea. Although the river was shallow, it held just enough water to accommodate the draft of the treasure-laden ship. Into this vast inland sea sailed the Spanish vessel a few days later, the captains and divers constantly on the lookout for more oyster beds.

For two weeks, the Spaniards sailed around this inland sea, only to discover it was little more than a shallow accumulation of overflow from the river and contained no oyster beds. Deciding to return to the gulf, Iturbe navigated the vessel back to the approximate location where it entered this sea, only to discover that a low ridge of land now separated the body of water from the river channel as a result of the dropping water level. The vessel was hopelessly landlocked with no chance of returning to the ocean.

According to geologists, it was not uncommon for the Colorado River to overflow its banks, contributing to the formation of large inland bodies of water such as southern California's Salton Sea and the one encountered by the Spaniards. The scientists also explain that earthquakes regularly occurred in this region, and still do today. The shifting of the continental plate here created significant changes in the topography then, as now. During one major earthquake that occurred around the time of Iturbe's visit, the channel of the Colorado River shifted eastward perhaps as much as fifty or more miles to its present location, leaving behind a landlocked body of water. This low desert region of southern California, in fact, straddles the famous San Andreas Fault, one of the most active earthquake regions in North America.

Convinced he could find another route to the gulf, Iturbe sailed around the shallow sea once again only to return to the same location days later. Not only was the ship trapped with no chance of reaching the Gulf of Mexico, the intense evaporation taking place in this extremely arid region was lowering the level of the already shallow inland sea at a rapid rate. A few days later, the ship's hull came to rest on the sandy bottom of the lake and began listing to one side as the waters continued to recede.

Finally realizing the hopelessness of their situation, the captains, crew, soldiers, and divers gathered up what possessions they could carry, abandoned the stranded ship with its store of precious pearls, and struck out across the sandy plain toward the Gulf of Mexico. Four months later, those who survived starvation, thirst, exposure, snakebite, and Indian attack were picked up by a Spanish galleon near the present-day city of Guaymas in the Mexican state of Sonora.

As the rescued Spaniards were being transported back to Acapulco, Iturbe's ship rested firmly at a severe angle on the now dry, windswept desert landscape hundreds of miles to the north. The constant winds rent the canvas sails to mere tatters and caused the drifting, saltating sand to accumulate nearly to the gunwales. Deep within the hold, a fortune in fine pearls reposed in wooden casks and clay pots now lightly covered with a fine dust. For two centuries the treasure-filled vessel lay thus, sometimes hidden by the drifting sands, sometimes partially exposed.

Following the end of the Civil War, thousands of Americans began making their way west, migrating from the battle-scarred grounds of the south and east to a land of economic promise on and near the Pacific coast of California. One of the many routes traveled by these newcomers bisected the Colorado Desert in Southern California. It was a hazardous journey, to be sure, but one that saved many miles and days. On reaching the port and industrial cities in the southern part of the Golden Bear State, some of these travelers reported a most bizarre encounter: the remains of what appeared to be a Spanish sailing vessel resting on the desert floor, at least one of its masts pointing skyward. During the last thirty-five years of the nineteenth century, hundreds of such sightings were recorded.

Time passed, and eventually the real story of the ship in the middle of southern California's Colorado Desert became known. In search of the rich cargo of pearls, dozens of expeditions ranged into the arid region between the Colorado River and the Vallecito Mountains in search of the vessel. In spite of many quests, several of them well-organized and funded, the ship could not be found. Some claimed it was buried under the desert sands, others insisted it never existed. Some were convinced the ship was haunted and only appeared during certain times of the year.

During the 1880s, more and more prospectors entered the Colorado Desert region of southern California to search for signs of gold and silver in the rock outcrops that dotted the environment. On returning to a town for supplies, a number of these prospectors mentioned spotting the remains of a ship out in the middle of the barren desert. For a variety of reasons, they were unable to investigate it: it was too far away; they were low on water; they weren't convinced it held any promise.

One old-timer who spent the better part of each year prospecting in the area claimed he camped on the rotted deck of the ship for several days but saw nothing interesting. He was unaware of the cargo of pearls

Dust devils churn in this mysterious (and probably doctored) photo of the California desert in 1921. Somewhere beneath the sand lies a seventeenth-century Spanish ship loaded with pearls. Library of Congress

stored in the hold of the vessel, presumably filled with sand by now. Many years later when the old man was informed of the great treasure inside the ship, he returned to the region several times but was unable to relocate the vessel.

In 1892, a party of prospectors traveling near southern California's Superstition Mountain, located eighteen miles southwest of the southern tip of the Salton Sea, discovered a long pole lying partially buried on the desert floor. One of the members of the party identified the object as a ship's mast. Another recalled the tale of the lost treasure ship supposedly located in that very desert. For the next two days, the prospectors explored the area in search of the ship but nothing could be found. They finally gave up and assumed the vessel was long buried under one of the many high dunes found there.

In 1915, an elderly Yuma Indian walked into the desert town of Indio and tried to purchase some food with a handful of small round stones. During the transaction, the storekeeper realized the stones were pearls, and exquisite ones at that. He asked where they came from, and in a long and rambling explanation, the Indian spoke of a journey of many days he just completed across the desert from some sixty miles to the southeast. During his travels, he said, he came to a large and strangely built "wooden house" mostly covered by sand. Inside this house, he said, he found many wooden cases, each of which was filled with the small, round, rose- and cream-colored stones.

Within minutes, the Indian's story was circulating around the town. A group of citizens banded together and offered the old man several hundred dollars if he would lead them to the "wooden house" of which he spoke. The Indian agreed, was paid, and accepted an invitation to sleep that night at the home of one of the investors. By dawn, however, the Indian had vanished and was never seen again.

As recently as 1999, backpackers, hunters, and trail bikers have returned from deep within the Colorado Desert of southern California with stories of finding the exposed bow or stern of an old sailing vessel. None were aware of the story of Iturbe's lost treasure-filled ship. Some, on learning the tale of the cargo of pearls, attempted to relocate the ship but were never successful.

Someday, the desert winds may again uncover the lost treasure ship of the desert and some fortunate hiker or rock hunter may discover the store of valuable pearls lying within, a fortune that today would equal the wealth of several countries.

LOST SPANISH GOLD MINE
ON THE COSSATOT RIVER

The annals of American history are filled with references to early Spanish settlement, missionary activity, agricultural development, and mining. Farms, ranches, and mines developed and worked by Spanish newcomers to the American South, Southwest, and West were in full and productive operation two centuries before westward expansion offered opportunities for tens of thousands of Americans. As a result of a number of factors—drought, Indian uprisings, shortage of manpower, political decisions—the Spanish gradually retreated from the American landscape and were forced to abandon productive fields and mines. In many cases, the mining of gold, silver, and other precious metals was documented, but now and then one encounters evidence of the Spanish quest for mineral riches in places shrouded in mystery. One such puzzle exists in southwestern Arkansas along the floodplain of the Cossatot River. From this part of the country comes a perplexing tale related to what was apparently a very productive gold mine that has been lost and found several times, and one that continues to baffle hopeful treasure hunters to this day.

In southwestern Arkansas, the Cossatot River flows out of the Ouachita Mountains and onto a fairly level plain where it eventually confluences with the Little River. Along its route, the Cossatot ranges from dangerous cascades and rapids to smooth, gentle flow. This river has been described in the literature as moody, and the name comes from an Indian word that translates to "skull-crusher." Today, the Cossatot affords a serious challenge to brave kayakers and canoeists who attempt its rapids and cascades in search of adventure.

In making its way downslope, the Cossatot River, for hundreds of thousands of years, has carved relentlessly through the soft sandstone layers that make up the bulk of the Ouachita Mountains. Here and there along the way, the river erosion has exposed the underlying igneous intrusive rock, remnants of eons-old volcanic activity that once dominated this region. During one of these ancient volcanic episodes, seams of gold formed in the cracks and fissures of the newly formed granite deep below the surface. During the millennia that followed, sea waters intruded into the area, covering the volcanic landscapes and depositing layer upon layer of sedimentary rock atop them. With the passage of time, the sea retreated and the layers of sandstone were squeezed and folded upward to altitudes that some geologists claim rivaled those found today in the Rocky Mountains. During this tectonic activity, the granite with its seams of gold was pushed closer to the surface.

Several streams such as the Cossatot flowed from the higher elevations toward the Gulf of Mexico some four hundred miles away, and in doing so effectively cut through the thick deposits of sandstone, exposing both granite and gold. In Sevier County, Arkansas, the Cossatot River incised deep into the sandstone layers and exposed sections of granite in which the Spanish explorers under the command of DeSoto discovered gold. Archaeological evidence reveals that the Spanish conducted mining activities throughout much of this area as well as in portions of the Ozark Mountains to the north. Both mining and expeditionary artifacts from that period are still found today. Although documentation is sketchy to nonexistent, many believe that the gold taken from this region was smelted, formed into ingots, and shipped back to Spain to be deposited in the treasury.

Although apparently productive, the gold mine adjacent to the Cossatot River was eventually abandoned by the Spaniards, who left behind a mystery that lives on today in both fact and legend.

Just prior to the Civil War, Dr. Ferdinand Smith brought his family to Sevier County, Arkansas, from Frankford, Missouri. The Smith family settled along the rugged forested bottoms of the Cossatot River where they cleared some land and planted crops. The reasons for Dr. Smith's move to Arkansas have been debated, but some suggest he was forced to depart Missouri because of the unexplained deaths of several of his patients. Because the few residents of Sevier County had no physician, Dr. Smith was welcomed and no questions were asked. Dr. Smith proved to be popular among the residents, making himself available to treat the sick and injured. More often than not he was paid with eggs, chickens, hams, and garden produce.

Dr. Smith possessed a keen interest in history and he found the local residents happy to talk with him about what they knew of the region's past. In this manner, he learned a fascinating tale about a rich lost gold mine located some distance upstream along the Cossatot River. This mine was also linked to the occasional appearance of a mysterious, blonde, Spanish-speaking woman who traveled in the company of Indians.

A few decades prior to the arrival of the Choctaw Indians in southwestern Arkansas, a trading post had been established at a location now known as Lockesburg. The post stocked a supply of clothing, tools, and food that was sold or traded for furs. The post served mostly the hunters and trappers who frequented the region, and later the few farmers who moved into the area.

According to the legend, approximately once every month a tall, blonde, fair-skinned woman accompanied by several young Choctaw Indians arrived at the trading post. According to those who saw her, she was dressed in leather garments and adorned with gold jewelry of rustic design and manufacture. She always rode to the trading post on a white horse, the Indians following behind on foot. It was apparent to all that the Indians were subservient to her and responded to her commands without hesitation. During her visits, the blonde woman would purchase essential foodstuffs and occasionally mining tools such as picks and shovels. She invariably paid with pieces of gold of the purest grade. On the rare occasions when the woman spoke, the language was Spanish laden with a heavy Castilian dialect. When she was asked where she obtained her gold she remained mute. Her Indian companions also refused to respond to similar questions. When her business at the trading post was completed, she mounted her horse and rode away, followed by the Indians who carried her purchases. Several attempts were made to follow the mysterious blonde woman, but she always managed to elude her trackers.

Now and then, someone would meet the strange woman and her escort returning from the trading post along a trail that eventually became a portion of the Fort Towson Road. On the few occasions when she was followed, she was observed entering Pig Pen Bottoms, a snake-infested, briar-matted section of the floodplain lying west of the Cossatot River. One observer told some men gathered at the trading post what he had seen, and before long a small expedition was formed to go in search of what they believed was a lost gold mine somewhere in the bottoms. The group was unable to locate an entrance into the dense, forbidding area, so they forced their way through underbrush and creepers. Once inside, however, they became disoriented and wandered for hours before finding a way out. They were all scratched and bleeding from the briars and covered with ticks. One member was bitten by a snake and suffered from delirium and swelling. Two hours past midnight, the party returned to the trading post where they reported the failure of their mission. The incident apparently made the blonde woman cautious, for neither she nor her Indian escorts were ever seen again. In recent years, Dr. Smith learned, local residents had reported spotting the ghostlike figure of a woman astride a white horse riding along the Cossatot River bottoms.

Fascinated with the possibility of locating the legendary lost mine associated with the blonde woman, Dr. Smith purchased a large parcel of land south of Rolling Shoals Ford on the Cossatot River. Pig Pen Bottoms was located between the ford and Smith's farm, and a large, dense thicket of briars, brush, and trees extended from the bottoms onto his property. Somewhere inside the thicket, Smith reasoned, would be found the lost gold mine.

Smith employed several men to clear brush so that this part of the bottoms could be placed into production. When the last of the huge expanse of vegetation was removed, a very old mine shaft was discovered in an outcrop of granite barely exposed above the silty deposition of the floodplain. The shaft was nearly vertical and, judging from several large piles of talus lying near the entrance, had been extensively excavated. Peering down into the shaft, Smith could see a number of very old and rotting timber supports. When he had one of his laborers lowered into the mine, he found that it was filled with water to within thirty feet of the surface.

For several years the lower section of the shaft remained inaccessible to those who were curious about what might be found there, who longed to explore its extent in search of the vein of gold and resume mining it. Then, during the mid-1920s, a severe drought struck this portion of Arkansas. The Cossatot River dried up to become a mere trickle, and the water tables in the area dropped dramatically. The water level in the old shaft had receded and inspired a group of men to attempt an entry.

Using ropes, two men carrying shovels and lanterns were lowered into the shaft. As they descended the ancient tunnel, they observed thick, rotting support timbers throughout. At around seventy-five feet, one of the men found a large, heavy hammer wedged between a support timber and the rock wall. At one hundred feet, they encountered water and were unable to proceed any further.

When they were hauled back to the surface, the hammer was passed around, and one of the men who examined it noted that tiny flecks of gold were adhered to the surface of the head. The hammer was later identified as having been cast in the city of Seville, Spain, during the sixteenth century, providing support for the notion that the mine was likely worked by early Spanish visitors to the area.

The deeper recesses of the mine shaft remained elusive to those who wanted to explore it until a second drought set in during the early part of 1927. This time, the water in the shaft was even lower than before, and a group of boys familiar with the tale of the lost mine made a descent. This time, there was no water at the bottom of the mine to halt their progress, and they lowered themselves to just over 125 feet where they encountered a thick deposit of silt, the fine soil that had been carried into the shaft during the many floods that had occurred during the previous centuries.

For nearly two weeks, the boys, sometimes accompanied by relatives, filled buckets with the silt and hauled them to the surface. As the work proceeded, the diggers found several more ancient mining tools, each bearing the mark of Spanish origin. Optimism grew, but as it did, the rain began to fall.

After two days of heavy rains, the diggers abandoned their quest to return home and wait out the storm. It was not to be, for the rains falling on the region were only the beginning of a long series of severe thunderstorms that struck Arkansas, Texas, and Louisiana and eventually gave rise to what has become known as the Great Flood of 1927. Within a few days, Pig Pen Bottoms was under water as the Cossatot River overflowed its banks and spilled across the floodplain on which the mine was located.

The river raged, and weeks later when it finally receded back to its channel, the surrounding landscape had been changed so much that it was barely recognizable. For many miles along the Cossatot, the floodplain received a new, thick deposit of rich river silt. This extremely fertile sediment, so valued by farmers, completely covered over the old mine shaft as well as the granite outcrop. When the diggers returned to the area to resume excavation, they were unable to find it. It was only after several more years passed that the outcrop was finally relocated under three feet of sediment. The entire mine shaft had been filled to the top with silt.

Over the years, several different groups formed to re-excavate the shaft but none was successful. Water was a constant problem. No sooner would some progress be made in unplugging the shaft than the spring rains would arrive bringing more flood waters. When the river was not flooding, the high water table inside the mine kept the diggers from reaching the vein of gold.

Today, there are several people who claim to know the exact location of the old Spanish mine shaft. A few professional treasure hunters and salvors who have expressed interest in reopening the mine are concerned about the past failures and the troublesome water that fills it. Most researchers are convinced gold will be found at the end of the long tunnel but insist there is little likelihood of retrieving any. A pair of civil engineers who visited the site in 1999 have stated that reopening the shaft is definitely within the realm of possibility and when last heard from were making plans to investigate the possibilities of securing a mining claim.

A few of the more superstitious residents of nearby Gillham and Lockesburg, Arkansas, have suggested that a curse was placed on the mine by the mysterious blonde woman who lived here during the midnineteenth century. Whenever anyone gets near the gold at the bottom of the mine shaft, they claim, the Cossatot River rises out of its banks to thwart the efforts.

Curse or not, the lost gold mine of the Cossatot River has attracted the attention of several experienced treasure recovery specialists. The answer to retrieving the gold, they claim, lies in technology. The residents respond that the river has no respect for technology and in the end will be the victor.

THE LOST GOLD MINE IN
THE UINTAH MOUNTAINS

This odd tale involves the unlikely juxtapositioning of elements from three radically different cultures—Spanish, Mormon, and Ute Indian—all revolving around fabulously rich gold mines in Utah's Uintah Mountains. These mines yielded tons of rich gold ore for years, were closed off, subsequently lost, rediscovered, and then lost again.

During most of the Spanish reign of what is now a considerable portion of the western United States, the mining of gold and silver involving hundreds, if not thousands, of Spaniards, Mexicans, and Indians was conducted in a variety of locations throughout the Rocky Mountains from New Mexico and Arizona almost to the Canadian border. Once the ore was dug from the vein, it was extracted from the rock matrix, melted down, refined, and poured into molds to form ingots. The ingots, loaded onto mules or burros, were relatively easy to transport the hundreds of miles south to government and church headquarters in Mexico City. There, the bullion was recorded, shipped to the east coast, normally to the city of Vera Cruz, loaded onto ships, and carried across the Atlantic Ocean to Spain. Some of it went into the Spanish treasury, a portion was allocated to the church, and some was used to support military and colonial efforts throughout parts of Europe, Africa, and the high seas.

The mining of gold and silver ore in the Rocky Mountains was often accomplished in opposition to the wishes of local Indian tribes. In several instances where the Indians resisted the Spanish intrusion, they were encountered, conquered, and often enslaved to perform the hard labor in the mines. In other cases, hostile tribes, most often fewer in numbers than the Spanish forces, were simply evicted from their lands, or killed off. Once in a while, however, the Spanish encountered Indian tribes who resisted domination by the invaders and fought back, often with success.

Dozens of mines yielding gold and silver were opened and operated by the Spanish in the Uintah Mountains in what is today the state of Utah. So rich were these mines that hundreds of Spaniards were assigned to the region—laborers, engineers, soldiers, and missionaries. It proved to be a highly profitable investment of men and energy, and officials in Mexico City looked with keen favor upon the wealthy and productive mines, eagerly anticipating the shipments of bullion that arrived several times each year.

On first entering the Uintah Mountains during prospecting forays, the Spanish encountered initial resistance from the Ute Indians. The Uintahs were part of the Ute homelands and hunting grounds, and the tribe resented the intrusion of the Europeans. The newcomers killed off much of the wild game for food and trespassed upon sacred lands. When the Utes retaliated, many of them were captured, chained together, and put to work in the mines. Those who escaped the domination of the Spaniards waged continuous and savage warfare against them at every opportunity. As a result, life for the Spaniards in the Uintah Mountains was precarious and far from secure. The Utes successfully preyed on Spanish prospecting and hunting parties, often killing a half-dozen or more Spaniards at a time. The ruthless Indians occasionally perched on mountain crests overlooking the mining operations, lobbing arrows and lances into the midst of the miners and soldiers. The encounters occurred year after year.

Each year as the winter season approached, the biting cold and deep snow of the Uintah Mountains forced the Spaniards to close down the mines temporarily. Many of the miners and mule drivers returned to Mexico as escorts for the gold-laden pack train, but several of the officers and priests bided their time in places such as Santa Fe or Taos where they patronized the taverns. Here they would rest while they awaited the spring thaws, at which time they would return to the mines and resume excavating the gold.

During mid-autumn of 1680, heavy snows began falling in a canyon in the Uintah Mountains that was the site of several productive gold mines. Tons of rich gold had been dug from the mountains here and shipped to Mexico City, and there seemed to be no end to the thick veins. As the military officers directed the shutting down of the mines and prepared for the departure to Mexico City, the accumulated gold ingots were stuffed into stout leather panniers and strapped to pack saddles on twenty burros. After all were ready, the long pack train, preceded and followed by miners, engineers, missionaries, and a few soldiers on foot, wound its way slowly down the steep trail that led out of the canyon.

Hours later when the party entered a broad meadow at the mouth of the canyon, it was set upon by a large contingent of Utes who came streaming out of the nearby forest on horseback and afoot, all brandishing bows and arrows, lances, war clubs, tomahawks, and knives. Caught completely by surprise and unprepared for the attack, the Spaniards were all slaughtered within minutes.

When the Utes finished scalping and mutilating the corpses, they rounded up all of the Spaniards' horses and drove them away to their village. The burros, each carrying a heavy load of gold ingots, were led back up the canyon toward the mines. Several of the dead Spaniards were loaded onto horses and likewise returned to the mines. There, the Utes removed the packs of gold and carried them into one of the abandoned mine shafts where they were dumped. Atop the gold were placed the bodies. Following this, the Indians stacked rocks over the entrances to all of the mines and left the canyon.

In 1847, a large party of Mormons arrived at what is now Salt Lake City, located just to the west of the Uintah Mountains. Led by Brigham Young, these newcomers, all members of the young religious sect, had been taught to believe that the American Indian tribes were descended from the Lost Tribes of Israel. As a result, insisted the Mormons, the Indians were to be treated with respect, a treatment they received from no other whites they encountered. Young, a shrewd and manipulative leader, possessed motivations that went far beyond religious considerations. He was convinced that if he patronized the local Indians the Mormons would be less likely to suffer from depredations on their livestock. Young also planned to enlist the Indians in the fights with anti-Mormon forces that occasionally plagued the members of the religion.

Within only a few years, Salt Lake City grew into a thriving and prosperous city located along the trail of many westbound wagon trains. Commerce was brisk as the Mormons traded important goods and supplies to the immigrants. A number of the Salt Lake City merchants insisted that payment for goods be made in gold. During one transaction between a storekeeper and a group of Oregon-bound migrants, a Ute Indian sub-chief stood nearby and observed the transaction. The Indian, whose name was Yahkira, was fascinated by the use of gold as a bartering element for white men. Several weeks later when Yahkira was visiting

Mormon leader Brigham Young, one of a handful of people who knew the whereabouts of a mine containing Spanish gold ingots. Library of Congress

with Brigham Young, he told the Mormon leader that, because his white people were friendly toward the Utes and treated them fairly, he would lead him to a place in the nearby mountains where gold, such as that used in the transactions he witnessed, could be found in great quantities. Young, perceiving a need for wealth in his growing community, eagerly agreed to accompany Yahkira. About one week later, the two men rode their horses eastward into the heart of the Uintah Mountains, nearly one hundred miles away.

As Yahkira led Young up the steep trail toward a remote canyon, he related an amazing story. He told Young of the beginnings of the mining operations in this canyon by the Spanish and how they had enslaved and killed many members of the Ute tribe. He explained how the Indians, on observing the Spaniards prepare to leave the mountains for another winter, laid in wait for them at the mouth of this very canyon, attacking and killing every one of them. He spoke of how the gold-laden burros were then led back to the mines and hundreds of ingots returned to the shaft from whence they came. He told of how the Indians placed the bodies of the dead Spaniards atop the gold. Yahkira explained to the Mormon how the Utes treasured and protected their mountain stronghold and resented the trespass of the arrogant Spaniards.

Yahkira led Young directly to the mine shaft in which the gold ingots had been hidden. Beneath the skeletons of nearly a dozen men lay more gold ingots than Young could count. While they were inside the old mine, Yahkira exacted a promise from Young that he was never to reveal the secret location of the gold except to those designated by the Mormon leader to travel to the mine to retrieve the bullion.

In 1853, a man named Thomas Rhoads, a devout Mormon, arrived in Salt Lake City to make it his home. Rhoads was a surveyor and miner by profession and had made an impressive fortune in the California gold fields. Now that he had money and was not required to work full time to earn a living, Rhoads decided that he would commit himself more fully to his church. He solicited and received a meeting with Brigham Young wherein he related his successful experience as a miner and described his particular skills. Taking Rhoads into his private chambers, Young told him about the existence of the old Spanish mines in the Uintah Mountains and explained the church's need for this wealth.

Young made Rhoads take an oath never to reveal the location of the old gold mines. Several days later and in the company of three Indian guides, Rhoads departed for the secret canyon in the Uintah Mountains. Just short of two weeks later, Rhoads returned to Salt Lake City leading a pack mule loaded down with chunks of gold dug from a vein found in one of the mines. In later years, Rhoads told an interviewer that the vein he found was so rich that he was able to chop out enough of the ore to fill two saddlebags without ever moving from one spot. The supply of gold in the vein, he said, was inexhaustible. Rhoads made dozens of trips into the Uintahs over the next few years, each time returning with several mule loads of ore.

The secret location of the gold mines was known only to Brigham Young, Thomas Rhoads, Yahkira, and a handful of other Ute sub-chiefs. The gold retrieval operations were handled clandestinely because Young did not wish any information about the source of the ore spread about. The last thing he desired was a gold rush bringing outsiders into his Mormon empire.

Entrusting only a few close associates, Young directed the construction of a small smelter that was intended to turn the gold ore into coins to be used by his followers. Additionally, some of the gold that was carried from the Uintah Mountains to Salt Lake City was fashioned into cups, chalices, candleholders, and other items that can still be seen inside the city's temple today.

Every now and then when Rhoads traveled to the gold mines in the Uintah Mountains, he would take along his young son, Caleb. Caleb never swore an oath of secrecy, and the Utes tolerated his presence in the mountains because of his youth. As the boy grew older, however, he began to learn about and appreciate the value of gold. When he turned eighteen, he began slipping into the canyon on his own and taking some of the ore for himself.

Time rolled on, and eventually Brigham Young and Thomas Rhoads passed away. When the elder Rhoads died in 1869, Caleb was called before the church leaders and instructed to continue his father's work retrieving the gold from the Uintah Mountains and delivering it personally to the Mormon leaders. Caleb agreed to the arrangement, and was to serve the Mormon church in this position for many years. Aside from only a handful of Utes, all of whom were elderly, Caleb Rhoads was the only man who knew the location of the gold mines.

Unlike his father, Caleb Rhoads never swore an oath of secrecy relative to the gold mines in the Uintah Mountains. Also unlike his father, Rhoads never felt any obligation to the Mormon church outside of his gold-retrieving responsibilities. As he grew older and more infirm, Rhoads attempted to reveal the location of the mines to others on several occasions. Once in the mountains, however, the hopeful searchers became hopelessly lost and realized no success. There are rumors that Rhoads sketched three or four maps purporting to show the location of the secret canyon, but they have never been found. The manner in which Caleb Rhoads was compensated by the Mormon church has never been revealed. Some have suggested he was paid a handsome salary, but others suspect he simply kept some of the gold for himself. Whatever the case, Rhoads grew wealthy over the years, purchased a large ranch, and settled into being a successful rancher and landowner. When he died in 1905, Caleb Rhoads was considered to be one of the wealthiest men in the state of Utah.

With the passing of Caleb Rhoads went the knowledge of the location of the secret Spanish gold mines save for a few Ute sub-chiefs. During his final days, Rhoads attempted to provide some information about the location of the mines, but his descriptions were unintelligible.

Within a few months following the death of Caleb Rhoads, rumors of the extensive gold deposits in a secret canyon in the Uintah Mountains grew widespread. Miners, prospectors, adventurers, and treasure hunters arrived in the range in great numbers, all hopeful of striking it rich. A few found some small amount of gold, and an uncommonly high percentage found only death, many believe at the hands of the Ute Indians.

During the 1890s, two prospectors arrived in Salt Lake City seeking directions to the Uintah Mountains. They spent nearly a year in the range searching for gold, but most particularly, looking for the lost Spanish gold mines in the secret canyon. Months after they disappeared into the mountains, they were seen leaving, each man leading a mule carrying a heavy load. Days later, the two prospectors stopped at a ranch and asked permission to water their animals and themselves. During a conversation with the rancher, the two men admitted to finding the old Spanish gold mines in the Ute lands. At one point, one of the prospectors opened up a saddlebag and displayed the contents. It was filled with gold nuggets.

Over the next few years, the rancher reported that the same two men stopped at his ranch on other occasions, each time coming from the direction of the Uintah Mountains and transporting leather packs filled with gold. When asked about the location of the mines, the two men refused to discuss anything, stating only that they were convinced they had located the same deposits from which Thomas and Caleb Rhoads had obtained their ore.

One spring, the two prospectors were spotted riding into the Uintah Mountains to retrieve another load of gold, but no one saw them return. The rancher said the two men did not make their customary stop at his place, and he had an uneasy feeling they had encountered some bad luck in the range. Years later, the skeletons of two men were found deep in the mountain range. Many believed they were the remains of the two prospectors and that they had been killed by the Utes.

In 1956, a man named Clark Rhoads was hunting deer in a canyon in the Uintah Mountains when he claimed he accidentally found one of the lost gold mines. While searching a canyon for deer one winter, Rhoads crossed a set of bobcat tracks in the snow and followed them. The tracks led to an old mine shaft, the entrance of which was partially covered by large rocks. Curious, Rhoads wanted to enter the shaft and explore it, but he had no light. He decided to return the following summer. When he arrived months later, he explored the old shaft, finding several Spanish artifacts only a few dozen yards from the entrance. He noted that several yards inside, a section of the shaft had been filled in with dirt and rocks and he grew curious about why anyone would go to so much trouble. Intrigued by the color and composition of some of the rocks he found on the floor of the old shaft, he placed several in his pocket. After a few more minutes of exploring, he left. Weeks later, he had the rocks assayed and learned they contained a high gold content. Rhoads returned to the shaft the following year with the goal of removing the rock and dirt fill to see what might have been concealed. After laboring in the shaft for two days, he determined that the rock structure was dangerously unstable and that the roof could collapse at any time. Unwilling to risk his life and invest any more time and effort into the potential of finding gold, Rhoads left the canyon, never to return. (It was never determined whether or not Clark Rhoads was related to Thomas or Caleb.)

In 1988, two sixteen-year-old Ute Indian boys were found to be in the possession of six gold ingots, all of them formed in the style of early Spanish mining, and two of them bearing Spanish letters and symbols. When asked where they obtained the bars, the two youths told authorities they were taken from an old mine shaft in the Uintah Mountains, pulled from a pile that contained hundreds more. They refused to provide any more information, confessing they feared they might be killed by members of their tribe.

Legend persists even today that the secret canyon containing the old Spanish gold mines is still guarded and protected by the Ute Indians. It is a fact that treasure hunters who have entered the range in search of the lost canyon have been killed or simply disappeared. One fortune hunter was interviewed during the 1960s by a Salt Lake City newspaperman prior to leaving for the mountains. Weeks later, his decomposed body was found in the Uintahs. He had been shot through the skull. The Uintahs have recorded over two dozen unsolved murders during the past half-century.

For centuries, great amounts of gold have been taken from the secret Spanish mines in the Uintah Mountains, and the evidence suggests that much more remains, ever tempting the adventurous and courageous who seek to grow rich from it. The evidence also suggests that such a thing will not be easy to accomplish, and that the Ute Indians continue to exert an influence over the region.

THE LOST PADRE MINE

In extreme far west Texas, the Franklin Mountains bisect the border city of El Paso. This north-south trending range contains an impressive diversity of igneous and sedimentary rock. Fossil hunters comb the slopes of these mountains for the unique specimens found there. In addition, abundant evidence exists that precious metals such as gold and silver were formed in the mountain's igneous rock eons ago. And somewhere in this range, according to legend, lies one of the oldest and richest gold mines in all of North America, a mine associated with the Spanish priests who once held great power in this region over the Indians, and one that continues to mystify treasure hunters today.

During the sixteenth century, much of the American Southwest saw the arrival of the Spanish explorers. They came with the intention of inventorying this new land and its inhabitants, establishing settlements, farms, and ranches, and prospecting for mineral riches. Another important objective was the establishment of a mission church and living quarters for the priests. From here, holy men ranged out in search of souls to convert. Soon, a number of Catholic missions were founded along the Rio Grande from the Mexican border north throughout much of New Mexico.

In 1659, the Catholic Church oversaw the establishment and construction of a mission in the town of El Paso del Norte, now Juarez, Mexico. The mission was called Nuestra Senora de Guadalupe and stands today near the center of Ciudad Juarez, a thriving city boasting well over one million residents.

During the seventeenth century, however, this region along the Rio Grande was sparsely populated by a few small, poor Indian tribes and the mission settlements. During its formative time, El Paso del Norte served as a rest and supply stop for travelers, trappers, prospectors, soldiers, and entrepreneurs. The mission, as well as the adjacent buildings, were constructed using native materials and Indian labor. Although the Indians were regarded as converts by the church, they were treated little better than slaves who performed work for the priests. They were routinely whipped, chained, and starved. The Indians generally came from the tribes that settled along the flood plain of the Rio Grande, hunting game, gathering wild foods, and growing crops like corn.

Every morning during and following the construction of the mission, a small group of Jesuits, leading a number of Indians, crossed the river and hiked into a canyon in the Franklin Mountains. Here, the Indians were directed to dig gold ore from a rich seam that extended deep into the rock. The gold had been discovered by a priest months earlier who immediately reported it to the church officials. A short time later, the church ordered the Jesuits of the Nuestra Senora de Guadalupe mission to dig the gold, process it, and ship it to church headquarters in Mexico City. Thus, the coffers of the church would grow richer and the priests in El Paso del Norte would gain favor with their administrators.

When a significant amount of the gold-bearing rock had been dug from the vein, it was transported some distance back down the canyon and close to the Rio Grande where the ore was separated from the matrix using a crude arrastre. This done, the ore was melted and poured into molds, forming ingots. When several hundred of them were accumulated, approximately once every month, they were loaded onto burros and transported to Mexico City.

The legend states that every morning a priest climbed to the top of the mission tower and tolled the bell, summoning all of the other priests to worship. From this vantage point in the bell tower and in the light of the rising sun, it was said, one could see the opening to the padre's gold mine in the Franklin Mountains.

The activities associated with running the mission and the grounds, as well as the mining of the gold, continued uninterrupted for several years. During this time, virtually all of the Indians in the area had been converted to Christianity, sometimes voluntarily, often by force. The church prospered with its increasing inventory of converts and the accumulation of vast stores of gold.

One afternoon during 1680, a messenger arrived at the mission, weak and hungry from having ridden a great distance without stopping for food or water. The news he carried was not good. He warned the mission priests that the Pueblo Indians, who resided several days ride to the north, had revolted and were ranging along the Rio Grande killing every Spaniard and Catholic they came in contact with and driving away others in flight. The Pueblos had grown weary of the enslavement by the priests and the strict, unbending authority of the Catholic Church. The messenger, who barely escaped a massacre at the hands of the Pueblos, was warning everyone he encountered along the route south to Mexico. The Pueblos, under the leadership of Chief Cheetwah, were heading in the direction of the Nuestra Senora de Guadalupe mission.

Concerned about an impending attack, the mission priests gathered up all of the church valuables including gold chalices, vessels, candlesticks, crosses, platters, and ornaments of various descriptions. To this, they added more than two hundred burro loads of gold ingots that were awaiting shipment to Mexico City. After loading this great wealth onto the backs of some two hundred fifty burros, mules, and Indians, it was transported to the mine in the Franklin Mountains, carried deep into the shaft, and stacked against the walls. From the river, the Indians carried baskets loaded with red silt up to the mine and used it to fill the shaft. According to the legend, three of the priests were killed and their bodies buried in the shaft along with the treasure. Their spirits, so goes the tale, would forevermore guard against the possibility of anyone but the Spanish recovering the immense wealth that lay within. Following this, great care was taken to stack rocks in front of the entrance to the mine shaft in order to make it appear like the rest of the mountain.

For the next two years, the Spaniards alternately fought with and fled from the warring Pueblo Indians. During this period, the priests who had been associated with the operation of the mine fled to Mexico City, abandoning the mission.

Years passed, and the Pueblos were ultimately subdued by large forces of Spanish military which reclaimed all of the lost territory. When the region was declared safe, the church sent priests back into the region to continue their work. When a party of Jesuits arrived at the Nuestra Senora de Guadalupe mission in El Paso del Norte, one of their priorities was to reopen the gold mine, return all of the artifacts to the church, ship the gold ingots to Mexico City, and resume mining operations. Unfortunately, most of the priests who originally worked at the mission were dead and the rest had been transferred back to Spain. Using directions to the mine that had been provided by church officials, the newcomers became hopelessly confused and were never able to locate it. Although the new priests looked for the mine for several years, luck was not with them and they finally abandoned the search. Save for a few written notations pertaining to the operation of the mission, little reference to the rich gold mine and the cache of precious church artifacts could be found. During the next century, the matter was forgotten.

In 1882, a researcher working in the archives of the Catholic Church in Mexico City accidentally encountered a reference to an extremely rich lost gold mine located in the Franklin Mountains near what was now being called El Paso, Texas. The account described the caching of over two hundred burro loads of gold ingots and several more carrying valuable church artifacts. The mine shaft, according to the account, was filled in with red river silt and the entrance covered over with rocks. Fascinated at the possibility of so much wealth being buried in one place, the researcher, whose name is unknown, solicited a group of investors to finance his search and excavation. Their intention was to find the lost mine, retrieve the ingots and the church artifacts, and divide the treasure among themselves. This done, they intended to continue mining the gold from the rich vein described by the priests.

The researcher and his investors hired several experts, including a mining engineer, a geologist, and a hydrologist. Despite spending almost a year exploring the various canyons in the Franklin Mountains facing Mexico, they found nothing and eventually abandoned the project.

Several years later, a man named Robinson learned of the organized search for the lost mine and decided to find out all he could about it. In addition to acquiring information possessed by the earlier exploration team, Robinson encountered the tale about being able to view the entrance to the mine from the bell tower in the old mission in Juarez. Robinson visited the tower, and from this position located two or three canyons that had the potential of being the site of the mine.

After spending weeks hiking an area along the foothills of the Franklin Mountains to the banks of the Rio Grande, Robinson found evidence of a very old trail, one that led from the old mission into the heart of a large canyon. Recognizing it for the important clue that it presented, Robinson redoubled his efforts and spent more time searching for the mine.

Along one side of the canyon, Robinson noticed a pile of rock and debris that did not look as if it had been deposited naturally. It appeared that some of the rock in this particular location came from elsewhere and that it was mixed with what looked to Robinson like very old mine tailings. Beset with curiosity, Robinson laboriously dug away tons of the rock and discovered an opening to a manmade shaft. The shaft, he said, was filled with red dirt, a type of silt he later learned could only have come from the river hundreds of yards away.

Realizing that he was faced with a tremendous amount of work removing the silt from the mine shaft, Robinson returned to town and over the next few days secured a small amount of funding to support his effort. He hired a dozen laborers, led them to the opening, and put them to work digging out the dirt. Several yards of the shaft had been cleared when Robinson ran out of money. When he returned to El Paso to request more, he was turned down. Angered at the turn of events, Robinson returned to the mine and ordered his workers to refill the shaft and replace the rocks so no one else could find it. Following this, Robinson left town and was never seen again.

In 1901, one of the El Paso newspapers reported that a man named L. C. Criss had discovered what he called the Lost Padre Mine. According to the article, Criss had been searching for the mine for fifteen years based on some information he found in an old manuscript located in the Nuestra Senora de Guadalupe mission in Juarez. Among other descriptions he found in the account, Criss encountered one that stated that a person could climb from the mine to an adjacent ridge and look directly down onto the city of Juarez. The document also included an inventory of all of the church artifacts that had been taken to the mine to be hidden from the warring Pueblo Indians.

Like Robinson earlier, Criss found the pile of rocks that covered the entrance to the shaft. After removing them, he encountered the fill of red silt, as he expected. Using his own resources, Criss employed a team of laborers to excavate the dirt from the mine. Work progressed smoothly. When one hundred feet of the shaft had been cleared, the workers found several ancient Spanish tools, an anvil, several spikes, a pair of spurs, and a rotted boot. For several weeks, these items were placed on display at an El Paso business and were viewed by thousands.

Another few days passed and a total of 125 feet of the shaft had been opened up. At this point, the shaft came to a T, with each of the limbs leading away at ninety degree angles to the original shaft, the entrance to each of them walled up with adobe blocks. Selecting one of the shafts, Criss tore out the wall only to discover that this one was also filled with red river silt. Twenty feet of the dirt had been removed when Criss observed that the timbers supporting the weak, crumbling rock of the ceiling were rotted and coming apart. Concerned about the possibility of a cave-in, Criss ordered his laborers out of the mine. He invited two of them to travel with him by wagon to El Paso to purchase some shoring timbers to replace the old ones. Before leaving, he left instructions that no one was to enter the mine.

Once Criss was out of sight, however, one of the workers, a man named Cruz, was convinced they were only inches away from uncovering the fabled lost treasure of the padres. Grabbing a shovel, he crawled back into the shaft and resumed the excavation. He had been working no more than twenty minutes when the roof in this section of the mine caved in, killing him instantly and effectively sealing off the passageway.

When Criss returned with the timbers, he was stunned to learn of the death of Cruz. Shaken, he immediately canceled further work in the mine and told his workers he wished to take a few weeks off from this project. During this idle time, however, Criss ran out of funds. Although he made several attempts to obtain more, he was unsuccessful and was forced to abandon the project. Dejected, Criss covered up the entrance to the mine, it was told, by generating a small landslide on the slope above. Following this, he, like Robinson, departed El Paso and was never heard from again.

During the ensuing years, a number of other expeditions were conducted into the Franklin Mountains in search of the Lost Padre Mine, but all were unsuccessful. Nothing of any significance occurred until 1968, when a man named Martin, accompanied by his wife and an assistant, came to El Paso from California. In Martin's possession were old documents that described the location of the Lost Padre Mine, the amount of gold taken from it, the abandonment during the Pueblo uprising, and the subsequent caching of church artifacts along with hundreds of gold ingots. It also described the filling in of the shafts with red river dirt. This document, like Criss's, provided a complete inventory of all of the golden church valuables that had been placed inside the mine in 1680.

Martin made arrangements to lease a large backhoe, one capable of removing large sections of rock and dirt at a time. He also rented several other items of digging equipment, all of which he requested to be delivered to the site of the mine on the flank of the Franklin Mountains. With hundreds of El Paso residents from nearby subdivisions looking on, as well as television cameras and newspaper reporters recording the event, Martin directed the excavation of a portion of the slope.

The earth-moving machinery gouged a long, fifteen-foot-deep trench, one end of which came close to a well-traveled paved road. Hundreds of tons of rock were removed and pushed downslope. At one point during the excavation, Martin signaled the heavy equipment operators to halt, after which he climbed into the trench to inspect it. Using a small pickaxe, he chopped at one section of an exposed wall of rock, eventually removing enough material to reveal the rectangular outline of a mine shaft. The shaft was filled with fine red river silt. Before the end of the day, ten yards of the shaft had been cleared of the dirt.

That night, armed guards employed by Martin patrolled the area, re-pelling hordes of people interested in inspecting the promising mine shaft. Just after sunrise the next morning and just as more work on the shaft was about to commence, an official from the city of El Paso arrived, conducted an inspection of the area, and judged it to represent a hazard to nearby residents. The digging was halted immediately. Although Martin begged to be allowed to continue his search for the treasure and insisted he was very close to reaching it, he was refused. He was subsequently ordered to refill the trench and remove himself and the equipment from the site at once. Discouraged, Martin abandoned the project and returned to California. Additional requests by Martin over the next several months to resume digging were all denied by El Paso city officials. Finally, he gave up and never attempted to retrieve the treasure again.

During the 1980s, a professional treasure hunter who was convinced that an uncountable fortune in gold ingots and church artifacts did indeed lie deep within an old abandoned mine shaft in the Franklin Mountains, came to the area to examine the possibilities of renewing excavations. When he arrived, he discovered the area excavated by Martin was within only a few yards of houses and roads. It was further determined that any significant excavation into the mountain could potentially jeopardize the bedrock upon which the homes and other structures were perched.

That gold exists in the Franklin Mountains is not open to question. There are residents of El Paso today who relate stories of panning for gold along the slopes and in the canyons during and immediately after thunderstorms. Some who live in the numerous subdivisions that have crept into the foothills of the Franklins have reported finding small gold nuggets in their yards while gardening or working on their lawns.

The Franklin Mountains are rich in other minerals besides gold— silver had also been found in the range. During the early 1870s, a mining company surveying these mountains discovered two very old mine shafts, each about one hundred feet deep and each filled with the same kind of red river silt that was found in the Lost Padre Mine. After the dirt was removed from these two shafts, the miners were surprised to discover a three-foot-thick vein of silver in both. These shafts were located about two miles from the old Spanish mission in Juarez, and it led some to suspect that the padres mined the silver in addition to gold, although no records of such have ever been found.

During the 1990s, a few additional, very old shafts were found in the mountain range. Each of the passageways was clearly the work of human labor and hand held tools. In fact, in two of these shafts, tools of Spanish origin were found, but there was no evidence of gold or silver.

The legend of the Lost Padre Mine has been on the lips of treasure hunters and adventurers for over three centuries and is as enticing to many today as ever, continuing to lure the interested to El Paso and the Franklin Mountains, each explorer believing they will be the one to find a way to reach the lost treasure of the padres.

THE VICTORIO PEAK TREASURE

As improbable as it seems, a tiny, late eighteenth century Spanish settlement in a remote part of New Mexico's San Andres Mountain range became the setting of one of the most amazing treasure tales in North America. Victorio Peak, an unimposing granite pinnacle rising some five hundred feet above the surrounding Hembrillo Basin in present-day Sierra County, New Mexico, may hold one of the largest stores of treasure in history. This location is forbidding and dangerous, full of rattlesnakes during warm months, and it is difficult to penetrate owing to the fact that for the past several decades it has lain within the boundaries of White Sands Missile Range and is closed off by the United States government.

Within Victorio Peak lies a large cave, one not formed in the conventional manner by solutioning, but rather created as a result of a massive earthquake millions of years ago that split wide the interior of the mountain, creating a significant chamber within.

There is little doubt that lying within this extensive cave can be found several billion dollars' worth of gold ingots, gold and silver coins, golden religious artifacts, historical items, chests filled with jewelry, and much more. In addition to containing what most researchers agree is an uncountable fortune, Victorio Peak is a mysterious place, once deemed a holy site by Apache Indians. It continues to provide mysteries to this day with regard to the treasure lying within and it lures the adventurous and hopeful, each believing they will be the one to locate and recover the huge fortune.

Historical documentation, as well as abundant archaeological evidence, has proven that this region of New Mexico was visited by the followers of the Spanish explorer Francisco Vasquez de Coronado. It is also a fact that Coronado's miners searched for and discovered gold and silver in abundance in the San Andres Mountains as well as in nearby ranges.

Throughout this area, as well as in much of New Mexico, pieces of Spanish armor, spurs, weapons, and saddle and bridle fittings have been and are still being found.

Following the Spanish claim to this land in the new world came agents of the Catholic Church. Priests, including Jesuits, often accompanied the explorers and soldiers who traveled throughout the area. After the surveying and mapping of the region, church leaders were sent into the new lands to establish colonies and convert the resident Indians to Christianity. In the process, missions were constructed and agriculture and irrigation projects inflicted onto the landscape. During this early settlement period, vineyards were often established and fields of beans, corn, and squash were planted and harvested. Where valuable ore such as gold and silver was found, the church also became involved in mining, forcing the Indian converts to dig the ore from the rock matrix. For years, hundreds of pack trains bearing tens of thousands of ingots of gold and silver made the journey from these new settlements to church headquarters in Mexico City.

History is also clear on the fact that the Hembrillo Basin of the San Andres Mountains often served as a retreat and hideout for Apache war chief Victorio during the 1870s. Victorio kept his warriors busy raiding settlements up and down the nearby Rio Grande and commonly preyed on travelers and freight wagons. For the Apaches, the basin was easy to defend, and few travelers, hunters, or prospectors ever visited this remote location so near the dreaded Jornada del Muerto, the Route of the Dead Man, a waterless expanse that reportedly claimed the lives of hundreds since the time of the Spanish settlements.

During the late 1700s in France, a young man named Felipe LaRue joined a monastery. Though he was the son of a wealthy French nobleman, LaRue decided to live a life of poverty and denial. His goals were sincere, but LaRue found monastery life not to his liking and his tenure there was filled with dissent and protest against church authority. LaRue constantly challenged his superiors and questioned what he thought were bizarre and unreasonable religious policies. Deciding that the young, fiery monk needed to experience hardship, coupled with a desire to be rid of him, the church officials arranged to have him transferred to Mexico. Once there, he was assigned to work from dawn until dusk in the agricultural fields.

In Mexico, LaRue was happier than he had ever been, but his habit of challenging church policies and authority never waned. In truth, it became more intense. Because they regarded him as insubordinate, his superiors subjected him to additional labor, and from time to time he was tied to a post and lashed. The punishment only made LaRue angrier and even more resistant to church authority and doctrine.

Months passed, and LaRue grew weary of life in the fields. He often dreamed of journeying northward into the wild and unsettled lands he heard about from the traders and soldiers who occasionally visited the monastery. In this grand and expansive new country, thought LaRue, he could establish a colony of his own, a settlement where the residents could live and worship as they wished without the heavy-handed rule of the Catholic Church dictating what should be done and exacting unreasonable tithes from the poor.

Late one evening, LaRue assembled a contingent of some two dozen fellow monks who shared his ideals. Together, they stole several mules and a supply of provisions from the church and fled northward. Following weeks of tortuous travel across mountains and desert, the small party finally arrived at El Paso del Norte on the south bank of the Rio Grande, now Ciudad Juarez. Along the way, the small group enlisted a number of Indians who agreed to accompany them, and by the time they reached the town, their numbers had swelled to over thirty. In El Paso del Norte they purchased additional supplies, made inquiries about the land farther north, and departed.

Following another two weeks of the most difficult travel yet encountered, LaRue and his followers arrived at Hembrillo Basin. Here they found a good campsite, two freshwater springs, and abundant game. More important to LaRue, the location was far from well-traveled roads and offered the kind of isolation he required for his ideal colony. He was also concerned the church might make an attempt to find him and return him to the monastery for punishment.

The newly arrived colonists immediately set about constructing rude shelters of native stone and adobe and planting seeds of corn, beans, and squash. Hunters were sent into the nearby mountains to procure game, and others dug a narrow irrigation canal from the springs to the gardens.

During one hunting trip near the base of the granite peak that dominated the basin, LaRue and his men discovered a narrow opening in the rock and entered it. After following the wide crevice for several dozen yards, they came upon a thick, rich vein of gold ore. LaRue assigned two of the monks to excavate the gold, but when it was learned the vein was far more extensive than they first believed, he put nearly twenty men to the task of digging the precious ore from the mountain.

A crude arrastre was constructed to separate the gold from the quartz matrix. Following this process, the ore was melted down in a rudimentary smelter and poured into molds to form ingots. As the gold bars were accumulated, they were carried back into the passageway and stacked along one wall inside the cave.

Three years after LaRue fled the monastery in Mexico City, his whereabouts were finally learned from a dissident colonist who fled Hembrillo Basin and returned to the religous community. In addition to learning about the rogue colony, the church authorities were told of the extensive mining operation and the large and growing store of gold. The gold, claimed the authorities, belonged to the church, and they were determined to retrieve it. An expeditionary force was organized. Their orders were to travel to Hembrillo Basin, arrest LaRue and his followers, confiscate the gold, and return to Mexico City. Accompanying the soldiers on the expedition were half a dozen monks who were to remain at the colony and continue mining the gold for the glory of God.

Months later, LaRue's Indian scouts informed him of the approaching punitive expedition. The renegade monk immediately ordered the entrance to the gold mine closed and disguised and instructed his followers to deny the existence of any gold.

When the soldiers arrived, they rounded up and arrested every member of the colony. When LaRue was questioned about the gold, he denied any knowledge of it. He was stripped of his garments, laid across a rock, and lashed repeatedly, Bleeding badly, the flesh hanging in torn, bloody strips from his back, the monk steadfastly refused to admit the existence of the gold or the mine. After a full afternoon of severe torture, LaRue died.

Several of the colonists were also interrogated, subjected to whippings, and killed, but according to church documents, none revealed the location of the mine and the accumulated gold ingots, which by now undoubtedly numbered in the thousands. After a fruitless week, the soldiers chained the surviving colonists together and led them back to church headquarters in Mexico City where they would receive further punishment. The contingent of monks assigned to remain at Hembrillo Basin searched for weeks for the mine and the gold but had no success. Weeks later, they finally gave up and returned to the monastery.

During the 1870s, Apache Chief Victorio was the most feared Indian in southern New Mexico. He led raids out across the Jornada del Muerto attacking wagons, churches, mail coaches, immigrants, and villages. Following each raid, the Indians returned to their hideout at Hembrillo Basin. On several occasions, they returned with prisoners, whom the Apaches delighted in torturing for long hours before killing. The bodies, it was said, were carried into a cave inside the nearby peak and hung from makeshift crucifixes. It was also claimed that the booty taken during raids was stored inside the same cave.

On April 7, 1880, Hembrillo Basin was visited by a company of U.S. Army cavalry that engaged Victorio and his warriors in a pitched battle. The Indians were victorious, driving the soldiers from the area, and the rocky prominence that dominates the basin was thereafter known as Victorio Peak. Some historians have maintained that the reason the Indians fought so hard in defense of the site was because of the treasure and booty from raids they had stashed inside the mountain.

In November 1937, a small hunting party consisting of four men and one woman from the nearby town of Hatch arrived at Hembrillo Basin. The quarry was deer, and while the woman remained in camp, the men ranged out across the basin in search of game.

One of the hunters, Milton E. "Doc" Noss, decided to try his luck at Victorio Peak and was ascending one side of the mountain as a light rain began falling. Looking around for shelter, Noss made his way to a large overhanging rock under which he could wait out the rain. After squirming under the rock, he noticed a short distance away a rather small rectangular opening that appeared to lead straight down into the mountain. Ignoring the rain, Noss left the shelter, went over to the hole, and peered down into it. He noted that the shaft appeared to have been widened by human labor and that it was apparently very old. Deep in the hole at the limit of the fading light, he spotted a wooden pole with notches carved into it such that it served as a crude ladder.

When the rain stopped, Noss hiked back to camp, arriving before the other hunters. He told his wife, Ova, what he had found on the peak and asked her to refrain from telling the others. With Ova, Doc Noss made plans to return to Victorio Peak sometime in the near future to investigate the mysterious opening.

Two weeks later, Doc and Ova Noss returned to Hembrillo Basin and, carrying ropes and a flashlight, climbed the steep slope to the tiny opening. After tying the ropes off to a nearby boulder, Noss lowered himself into the dark shaft.

What Doc Noss found deep in the interior of Victorio Peak that afternoon has grown to be one the most controversial topics in American history, one that involves the discovery of fabulous wealth that exceeds the wildest imagination, one that led to murder, lawsuits, and the ultimate involvement of the United States Army and Air Force, the federal government, the government of the state of New Mexico, and a long list of prominent politicians and lawyers.

After descending down the steep shaft approximately sixty feet on the rope, Noss arrived at what he described as a large room. Using his flashlight, he found a number of petroglyphs on the walls of the room, some painted, some carved into the rock, all suggesting this spot had been visited by ancient Indians. Beyond this room, the shaft continued downward at a steep angle for another one hundred twenty-five feet before leveling out. Following the shaft, Noss eventually arrived at a large natural cave inside the mountain. Noss claimed this cave was large enough to accommodate a freight train and that several smaller "rooms" could be found along one side of it.

After proceeding into the cave for several feet, Noss stumbled over a skeleton. On examining it, he noticed that the wrists had been bound behind the back. Before leaving this room, he said, he found another twenty-seven skeletons, all bound and most of them secured to stakes that had been driven into the ground.

In one of the small rooms, Noss claimed, he found an old wooden Wells Fargo chest and a stack of items including very old guns, swords, and jewels, along with a number of church artifacts. In this same room he also found a box containing several dozen letters, the most recent one dated 1880. Next to this was a large pile of rotted leather sacks, each one containing gold nuggets. Noss claimed it would take sixty mules to carry all of the gold in the sacks. It was presumed that much of what Noss found had been stolen by the Apaches during some of their raids and cached here.

Noss stuffed his pockets full of gold nuggets, along with some gold coins and jewels he found. As he explored further into the large room, he encountered "thousands of bars of gold ingots stacked like cordwood." It may be that Noss stumbled upon the gold accumulated by Padre LaRue. He explored the cave for another half-hour before the batteries in his flashlight began growing weaker. Heavily laden with treasure, he climbed back to the surface with great difficulty and displayed the gold coins, nuggets, and jewels to Ova. Excitedly, he told her what he found in the cave. When she asked him why he didn't bring up any of the gold ingots, Noss explained that they each weighed about forty pounds. Ova chided her husband repeatedly about not returning with one of the gold bars, so Noss reentered the cave and, with the exertion of a great deal of effort, returned to the surface with one.

Over the next two years, Noss and his wife returned to Victorio Peak several times. During this period, Noss retrieved a total of eighty-eight gold ingots, each weighing between forty and eighty pounds. He also brought to the surface dozens of artifacts including golden church chalices, statuary, crosses, jewels, gold nuggets, and coins.

Now and then, Noss employed men to accompany him to the cave to help him retrieve the treasure. In 1963, Benny Samaniego admitted to an interviewer that, after entering the cave with Noss, he saw "stacks of gold bars, skeletons, armor, old guns, and statues." He stated that the skeletons looked as though they belonged to people who had been tied to stakes and left in the cave to die.

On another occasion, Noss hired a boy named Benny Sedillo. When he was interviewed years later, Sedillo described gold ingots stacked several feet high and spoke of how difficult it was to climb back out of the extremely narrow shaft. Sedillo also told his interviewer that Noss threatened to kill him if he ever told anyone of the existence of the treasure cave.

The two years of tedious labor transporting the heavy objects up through the narrow shaft caused Noss to consider enlarging it. He decided to dynamite the passage wider. Noss was inexperienced with explosives, and the resulting blast generated a cave-in which effectively sealed the opening with tons of debris and halted further entrance.

Noss was discouraged but not defeated. He began selling off some of the treasure he had accumulated in an attempt to raise money to get the shaft reopened. He took on a partner named Joe Andregg, who was able to arrange for the black market sale of much of the gold and artifacts.

During the subsequent months, Noss made several attempts to reopen the shaft, each one futile. During this time, Noss grew more frustrated and angry and fought increasingly with Ova. A short time later, they divorced.

On February 15, 1945, Noss filed a mining claim on Victorio Peak. For the next four years he worked at trying to remove the debris from the entrance. In 1949, he entered into a partnership with a man named Charley Ryan, a miner with a good reputation in the area. When Noss described the treasure cave to Ryan, along with the problem related to the blocked shaft, the miner was skeptical. To convince Ryan, Noss showed him the fifty-one gold ingots he still possessed and told him there were thousands more stacked in the cave. Convinced, Ryan told Noss he would be able to open the passageway.

As the two men began moving heavy mining equipment into Hembrillo Basin, Ova Noss filed a counter claim on the site. A short time later, a court ruled that until a final decision could be made, neither of the parties were allowed to enter the area.

Frustrated at the delay and Ova's attempt at gaining a share of the treasure, Noss began drinking heavily and fought often with Ryan. One evening as the two argued bitterly, Ryan shot Noss through the head, killing him instantly. Ryan was charged with murder but subsequently acquitted.

More time passed, and while Ova Noss maintained her claim on the Victorio Peak location, the U.S. government, through the power of eminent domain and insisting it needed the area for testing missiles, took possession of the region while expanding the boundaries of White Sands Missile Range (WSMR). On several occasions, Ova hired men, drove them to the peak, and attempted to reenter the shaft. Each time, they were escorted off the property by military officials.

Ova Noss wrote a number of irate letters to federal and state government agencies insisting she had a right to visit the property and work on her claim. Responses informed her she was not permitted to enter the land because of national security issues.

When she was told that members of the military were digging at her claim, Noss hired an attorney, who in turn contacted agents of the New Mexico state government. They queried White Sands Missile Range spokesman Colonel Jaffe who vehemently denied any excavation was taking place at the claim and insisted that no military personnel were involved in any activity related to the peak. Noss, convinced that Colonel Jaffe was lying, secured the services of a prominent attorney from Kansas City and instructed him to take her suit to the U.S. government.

While Noss, her attorney, and representatives of the federal government were involved in discussions, it was learned a second entrance into the treasure cave had been discovered a few years earlier. In 1958, an Air Force Captain named Fiege, along with another man, were exploring around Victorio Peak when they found a natural opening in one side of the mountain. The two men entered and followed the passageway for a few dozen yards when they came upon one hundred ingots of gold stacked along one wall. Noss also learned that in 1961, Fiege, along with three other Air Force officers assigned to WSMR, were granted permission by the U.S. military to recover any treasure they might find associated with the Noss claim.

On August 5, 1961, Fiege, his three partners, the commanding officer of WSMR, a secret service agent, and fourteen military policemen traveled to Victorio Peak but were allegedly unable to relocate the second opening. Fiege was subjected to a lie detector test regarding his discovery. He passed, and a short time later the U.S. government ordered a full-scale excavation undertaken at the peak in spite of the fact that the claim was still held by Ova Noss.

Noss did not trust the motives of the government, and she talked four men into sneaking into Hembrillo Basin and making an attempt to enter the shaft. They were promised a share of whatever treasure they might find. On October 26, 1961, the men crossed fences and hiked to Victorio Peak only to discover several U.S. Air Force and Army personnel digging into the blocked passageway. The four men were threatened at gunpoint and ordered to leave the area immediately.

Years later, several Fiege acquaintances informed authorities that the captain duped his superiors and later returned to the peak to retrieve a significant amount of the treasure.

Noss eventually convinced federal officials to halt the military-sponsored mining activities at her claim and honor her legal rights. During subsequent hearings, it was learned that the acting director of the Denver Mint had been granted permission by the U.S. Air Force Commander John G. Schinkle to dig for the Victorio Peak treasure. Missile Range spokesman Jaffe had been aware of the activities at the peak and purposely lied to any and all who inquired about the clandestine excavations. Following several rounds of court presentations and legal arguments, a judge decreed that all mining activities at the peak cease immediately.

In spite of this order, the Geddes Mining Company of Denver, contracted by the Denver Mint, was granted federal permission to dig into Victorio Peak during a designated period from July 13 to September 17, 1963, a time when no missile testing was going on. During this period, millions of tons of rock were removed from the top and sides of the mountain by heavy earth-moving equipment in an attempt to find additional entrances into the treasure chamber. None were found, and by the end of the period the scarred and stripped peak bore little resemblance to the natural granite pinnacle that previously existed.

The issue involving the alleged treasure deep inside Victorio Peak escalated and grew more complicated. Ova Noss was finally granted permission by the courts to enter the area and resume excavation. In 1972, however, prominent attorney F. Lee Bailey, joined by Watergate figure John Erlichmann and U.S. attorney John Mitchell, entered the fight for the treasure.

According to court documents, Bailey represented fifty clients who knew the location of a cave that contained one hundred tons of gold stacked inside. Ova Noss was not listed as one of the claimants.

In Albuquerque, New Mexico, on March 5, 1975, a federal judge declared that the United States Army had the right to deny permission to anyone wishing to excavate or conduct mining activities at Victorio Peak. The army was also given the authority to make special arrangements with any of the claimants as it saw fit. One such arrangement was made in 1977 when the army granted six different claimant groups two weeks to conduct a search. During the search period, a ground radar survey was undertaken and the result clearly revealed a large cave inside the peak precisely where Doc Noss said one was located. The radar survey also located the vertical entrance shaft filled with rock and debris. The two weeks passed without any of the parties gaining entrance to the treasure chamber.

The accumulated evidence suggests strongly that deep inside Victorio Peak lies an amazing treasure consisting of tons of gold ingots, dozens of golden church artifacts, uncountable sacks of gold nuggets, loot from numerous Indian raids, and perhaps much more. It is also believed that a significant portion of this treasure has been recovered by members of the U.S. Army and Air Force acting independently of military authority. Some researchers are convinced that the U.S. government formally, yet illegally, seized some amount of the treasure and tried to cover it up.

There is no doubt that the treasure existed. A large number of the ingots removed from the treasure cave by Doc Noss were viewed by others, even photographed. Additionally, employees of Doc Noss who entered the cave have spoken of viewing and handling artifacts and ingots and have signed affidavits to that effect.

The question remains: How much of the original treasure still lies inside Victorio Peak? The answer can only be conjectured, but many researchers are convinced most of the treasure, along with important historical artifacts, remains in the cave. The extent of pillage by members of the U.S. government may never be known, and individuals close to the excavation projects have suggested that the earth-moving activity conducted by the military may have had the effect of making entry into the treasure chamber more difficult. Today, military officials refuse to allow any excavation on or near the peak, and refuse to acknowledge the existence of the lost treasure within.

The mystery continues.

LOST SPANISH TREASURE
IN THE LAVA BEDS

During the eighteenth century, hundreds of pack trains transporting gold and silver bullion made their way from the numerous Spanish mines in southern Colorado to Mexico City. The mines, operated by the Spaniards, along with labor from enslaved Indians, produced the rich ore destined for the Spanish treasury in the mother country across the Atlantic Ocean. It is estimated that untold millions of dollars worth of gold and silver made the journey, but perhaps more interesting and compelling are the stories about the gold- and silver-laden pack trains that never reached their prescribed destination. To this day, the cargoes of many of them, in the form of gold and silver ingots, nuggets, and dust, remain hidden or lost at some location along the route as a result of some incident, or disaster.

One such disaster involved a mule train carrying hundreds of silver ingots from the mines near Durango. The treasure never made it past the treacherous lava beds found in west-central New Mexico. Here, the multi-million dollar cargo of silver ingots was buried and the drivers, along with the military escort, were attacked and slain by Indians. To this day, the treasure has never been recovered.

The year was 1770, and the military captain who was given command of the mule train carrying the silver to Mexico City many weeks to the south was feeling uneasy. He cast nervous glances into the distance, attempting to discern any threat to the pack train before it could surprise him. Dust rose in thick columns above the plodding mules as the pack train wound single-file along an ancient Indian trail that wove through the maze that was a seemingly endless landscape of basalt, the thick, black deposit of hardened lava. Other than the clopping of hooves and the occasional braying of the mules, the only sounds that could be heard were the cracks of long, black leather whips urging the animals forward and the accompanying curses of the mule drivers.

The captain was given the responsibility of escorting the treasure-laden mule train because of his record of success in previous similar assignments and his reputation as an efficient commander. He was regarded by his superiors as competent and trustworthy, and had proven his loyalty to the Spanish crown time and again. This was his third journey along the twisting, winding route through this portion of the desert Southwest. The silver ingots placed under his care always arrived safely at the Mexico City destination.

Previous trips along this same trail yielded evidence that Indians either lived in or passed through the region regularly, but none were ever encountered. The captain hoped he would find none on this trip, but he was unable to shake the uncomfortable feeling that bad luck was about to overtake them. His concern expanded as he led the long pack train into a narrow passageway that was the beginning of a route that wound through the tortuous maze in the lava beds. The sinuous corridor was so narrow that riders could reach out and touch the black basaltic walls on both sides, and the closed-in sensation made the mule drivers and the military escort apprehensive.

Men and animals had been on the trail for weeks since departing the extensive mining district near Durango. For days, they experienced heavy rains, thick mud, flood-swollen streams, then intense heat and severe sandstorms that reduced visibility to near zero. As the expedition approached the lava bed from the north, the bad weather gave way to clear skies, pleasant temperatures, and a gentle breeze. Rather than becoming heartened by the change, the mood of the riders darkened as they approached the lava beds. They became tentative, almost fearful, and the tension and worry among them was palpable.

Even the mules grew jumpy and nervous as, one by one, they entered the cramped canyon called the Narrows. Fourteen of the animals each carried over three hundred pounds of silver ingots, all packed tightly into stout leather panniers lashed tightly to wooden pack frames. Another six mules carried the food and supplies necessary for the long journey.

As the pack train traversed the narrow passageway, the captain recalled what he knew of it. The trail wound through the basaltic rock for well over two hundred yards before exiting into a wide grassy meadow ringed by the thick, dark volcanic rock. On the far side of the meadow to the south was the opening to another narrow access that wound for miles and would eventually take them out of the lava beds and into the wide open plains beyond. Once there, thought the captain, the worst part of the journey will be over. Though canyons and mountains would be encountered throughout the remainder of the trip, none would generate the amount of concern as did these troublesome routes encountered in the lava beds.

As the pack train streamed out of the Narrows onto the lush grasses of the spring-fed meadow, the captain ordered a temporary halt. He instructed the herders to unpack the mules, stash the packs in the shade of a nearby rock overhang, and turn the animals loose to graze among the grasses as the soldiers unsaddled their own horses and prepared for the respite.

Once the riding mounts joined the mules, the soldiers and herders retreated to the relative coolness of the rock shelter and built a small fire preparatory to preparing lunch. As one of the soldiers lifted a canteen to his lips, he spotted at least two dozen Indians filling the entrance of the passageway they would have to take in order to leave the lava beds. At the same time, several more Indians poured out of the narrow defile the pack train had just exited. Both groups of Indians stood in silence eyeing the Spaniards, arrows nocked on bowstrings, lances held at the ready. They were mostly naked save for breechcloths and moccasins. In addition to bow or lance, each carried a stone knife, and a few sported stone war clubs. Encircling the meadow, the high, steep walls of basalt served to remind that escape from this situation would be difficult, if not impossible.

For nearly an hour, the two opposing forces eyed each other from the distance, each group assessing strengths and weaknesses of the other. Suddenly, the Indians stationed at the north passageway loosed a volley of arrows into the Spaniards, wounding two. In retaliation, the soldiers raised and fired their heavy muskets into the Indians, killing several. Within seconds, the indigenes disappeared into the canyons.

As the captain and his officers pondered their few options, several Indians appeared on the basalt rim above the grassy meadow facing the rock overhang. In rapid succession, they fired arrows into the midst of the massed newcomers, forcing the Spaniards to retreat deeper into the rock shelter. From this safe position, however, the Spaniards were unable to return fire. They were, in fact, trapped.

For four days, the Spaniards huddled under the protection of the rock overhang. Each time a sentry ventured out to assess the position of the Indians, he spotted them clustered about the entrances to both of the passageways. Every now and then, a soldier would dash out from the rock overhang to fire his musket at the Indians, but he was invariably struck by arrows fired from the rim.

On the evening of the fourth day of hiding under the protective overhang, the captain noted the food supplies were running low. Soon, it would be necessary to fight their way out of the lava beds if they were to survive. The chances of escape were grim, and they all knew it.

Not wishing to be encumbered by thousands of pounds of silver ingots, the captain ordered the treasure buried. Soldiers and muleteers alike excavated a long narrow trench in the soft soil near the rear of the shelter. Into this they placed the ingots, still packed in the leather panniers, and then covered it up and smoothed it out. After examining the cache, the captain strode to the back wall of the shelter and, employing the tip of his sword, etched the image of a coiled snake into the wall of weathered basalt. The serpent was a traditional Spanish symbol indicating the presence of buried treasure nearby.

The next morning just before sunrise, the captain ordered the men to prepare their weapons and gather up any food or materials they wished to carry. A guard informed the captain that Indians continued to guard the entrances to the two passageways. The captain determined the only possibility of escape would be to fight their way out. After preparing his men, the captain issued an order, and the entire group, brandishing muskets, swords, knives, and even sticks, ran toward the south entrance in the hope of fighting their way out of the lava beds to the safety of the plains beyond.

Almost immediately, several of the Spaniards were felled by arrows and lances. The few that managed to reach the entrance to the narrow canyon were slaughtered within seconds by the Indians who awaited. Minutes later, the defenders were occupied with scalping their victims and taking what clothes they wanted. This done, the bodies were then hacked to pieces.

Taking the Spaniards' horses and mules, the Indians departed the meadow, leaving through the Narrows. Behind them, the blood-spattered grasses greeted the rising sun. Deep in the rock shelter, hundreds of silver ingots lay buried beneath just a few inches of soil.

Years passed, and the bones of the dead Spaniards that littered the south end of the grassy meadow in the lava beds had long been scattered or carried away by wild animals or gnawed by rodents. Here and there, partially covered by windblown sand and dust, pieces of Spanish armor, weaponry, and metal bridle and saddle fittings glinted in the sun.

With the coming of Anglo settlers in the region, it was inevitable that some would discover and explore the vast stretch of lava beds in this part of New Mexico. Cattlemen found the large grassy meadow and moved their livestock into it to graze on the rich grasses that grew there. Now and then, a cattleman or ranch hand would find a piece of rusted Spanish armor or a broken sword in the meadow, but the preoccupation of scraping out a living with livestock superceded any interest in the history or archaeology of the site. Sometimes while tending cattle in the grassy meadow, a cow hand would set up camp under the protective rock overhang, completely unaware of the rich treasure of silver ingots that lay just inches beneath the camp fire.

One of the prominent ranchers in this area, a man named Soloman Bilbo, married an Acoma Indian woman and from her learned the story of the massacre of the Spaniards in the lava beds, a tale handed down in the oral tradition over generations. Though the story was clouded from so many tellings over so many years, portions of the legend referred to the possibility that the Spanish trespassers had been carrying a fortune in silver from the mines in Colorado when they were attacked and killed. Intrigued by this tale and convinced a great treasure lay hidden somewhere in the lava beds, Bilbo searched long and hard but found nothing. Discouraged, and struggling with the infirmities of advancing age, he gave up looking for it.

Sometime during the 1930s, a young Indian arrived at the York Ranch in western New Mexico and politely asked for directions to the lava beds, specifically the entrance referred to as the Narrows. When the owner of the ranch asked the young man about his intentions, the Indian showed him an old map which purported to show the location of a huge cache of silver buried long ago in a grassy meadow located somewhere deep in the lava beds.

According to a story that had been handed down among his people, said the Indian, the Spanish officer in charge of the expedition transporting the treasure in silver ingots sketched a crude map of the location of the cache just before he led his men into the final, fatal battle. While searching the dead bodies of the slain, one of the Indians found the map, which had been drawn on a thick piece of parchment, and kept it. It remained in the family for many generations, eventually falling into the possession of the young Indian who carried it with him from his home in Arizona to western New Mexico. Prominently displayed on the map, according to a man who saw it, was the image of a coiled snake, the figure apparently pointing to the location of the buried silver.

With the help of three cow hands volunteered by the owner of the ranch, the Indian spent several days conducting a search of the lava beds, including the large grassy meadow. He found nothing, and the searchers never noticed the figure of a coiled snake scratched into the back wall of a rock shelter.

Several more years went by, and as the older generations passed and new ones came to this part of the country, the tale of the lost Spanish treasure in the lava beds was largely forgotten, except by a few.

One day during the 1950s, a young ranch hand rode into the head-quarters of the York Ranch seeking treatment for a rattlesnake bite. He was bitten in the calf of one leg, which had swollen so badly his boots and pants had to be cut off. The cow hand was hot with fever and deliri-ous. The foreman examined the bite and deemed it quite serious. He thought about driving the lad to the nearest town and a hospital, but it would have taken a full day. Instead, the foreman elected to put the cow hand on a cot to rest and kept him cool with wet compresses.

When he was able to take a break from his chores, the foreman sat at the young man's bedside, reapplying the compresses and examining his wound. Late evening of the second day, the cow hand regained con-sciousness but still carried a high fever. He recognized the foreman, who spooned some soup into his mouth. While he fed the youth, the foreman asked how he came to be bitten.

The cowboy, growing weaker, told the foreman that he had been looking after the cattle grazing in the grassy meadow in the lava beds. During a lunch break, he took shade in a nearby rock shelter while he ate a cold biscuit. Following a short nap, he rose and was preparing to get back to work when a large diamondback rattlesnake, lying unseen in the deep shade next to him, struck. When the foreman asked the cowboy about which rock shelter the event occurred in, he replied it was the one with the coiled snake scratched onto the back wall.

The foreman, an old-timer who had worked on a number of ranches in the area for four decades, was familiar with the story of the lost Spanish treasure in the lava beds. He decided that when the young man recovered from his snakebite, he would suggest the two of them ride out to the grassy meadow and look for the coiled snake. The treasure, ac-cording to the tale, lay buried in the ground near the foot of the wall.

The next day, the foreman went out to perform some chores. When he finished around lunch time, he walked into the house to check on the condition of the young cow hand and found him dead. During the next few days, the foreman saw to the burial of the young man and notified his relatives in Texas. At the first opportunity, he rode to the grassy meadow in the lava beds to search for the rock shelter and the figure of the coiled snake. He located several shelters, but was unable to find the one with the image. Though he searched off and on for years, he was never able to locate it.

In 1992, two men arrived in Albuquerque to sell rattlesnake venom to a dealer who in turn marketed it to companies that distributed it to research institutions. During a conversation with the dealer, the two related that their recent search for rattlesnakes took them to the lava beds of west-central New Mexico. Here, they claimed, they had great success, finding rattlesnakes in abundance. They knew they were going to have a profitable trip, they told the dealer, when they found the image of a coiled snake on the rear wall of a remote rock shelter.

Two years later, the dealer related this story to a friend who was familiar with the tale of the lost Spanish treasure. Realizing he had evidence that could lead him to a fabulous fortune in buried silver ingots, the dealer tried to locate the two snake hunters. The contact information he had for them was no longer accurate, and he was never able to track them down.

Today, the search for the lost Spanish treasure in the lava beds continues. In recent years, at least three expeditions have traveled to the area in search of the rock shelter containing the figure of the coiled serpent. To date, none have been successful.

LOST SPANISH TREASURE SHIP
ON BARKENTINE CREEK

September 1822 was remembered by Spanish seafarers for years afterward as "the time of the storms." During that month, an uncommonly high number of violent hurricanes formed, grew, and surged throughout the Atlantic Ocean and Caribbean Sea, with many of them ripping and tearing their way westward into the Gulf of Mexico and ultimately striking the Texas Gulf Coast in a line between Galveston and Corpus Christi. Many of the vessels that plied the Caribbean and Gulf waters during this time became victims of the storms. Others were confined to home ports along the eastern coast of Mexico until the dangers of the hurricane season ended.

During the first week of September when the waters of the Gulf of Mexico were relatively calm, a Spanish barkentine sailed out of the quiet harbor of Vera Cruz on the east coast of Mexico. The destination was Galveston, Texas, and the captain of the three-masted vessel intended to rendezvous with a number of other Spanish ships waiting there before embarking on the long voyage across the Atlantic Ocean to Spain. Each of the vessels carried a cargo of inestimable value: dozens of wooden casks filled to the top with gold and silver coins and ingots. This great wealth was intended for the Spanish treasury and to be used to support efforts to conquer and defend territories throughout the world and to fund further explorations and searches for precious metals and stones. Every available space in the barkentine's hold and much of the deck was filled with casks of riches, and the ship was weighted down so much that it rode dangerously low in the sea.

As the barkentine sailed parallel to the long, narrow Padre Island on its way toward Galveston, the normally placid waters of this part of the gulf began to swell and grow choppy. To the east, the skies were growing darker, more threatening. The captain of the barkentine, Diego Sotomayor, observed the changing conditions with interest, anticipation, and not a little concern. After about an hour of taking note of the sea and the weather, Sotomayor became convinced a major storm was approaching rapidly, one that might threaten his journey to Galveston harbor.

A short time later, the fierce winds generated menacing waves that washed across the deck, carrying men and equipment overboard and into the raging sea. The same winds began tearing the sails from the masts, and Sotomayor knew he must find shelter immediately or he could lose the ship, his crew, and the precious cargo.

The captain directed the crew to maneuver the barkentine through the narrow channel between Mustang Island and San Jose Island near present-day Corpus Christi, Texas. Once the channel was negotiated, he ordered his men to proceed along the somewhat calmer waters of the lagoon between the islands and the mainland. Believing he may have outwitted the storm, Sotomayor relaxed somewhat as he contemplated a late rendezvous at Galveston. Little did he know that most of the ships awaiting his arrival became victims of the same storm and had sunk to the bottom of the Gulf.

Sotomayor would never make it to Galveston. The low profile of San Jose Island and the shallow waters of the lagoon provided no protection from the growing storm whatsoever. As the powerful hurricane surged across the region, it swept over San Jose Island and nearly capsized the barkentine. As Sotomayor and his frightened crew fought for their lives, the storm raged inland, dropping torrents of rain in its wake and causing rivers and creeks to swell rapidly with runoff.

During a brief time of calmer winds, Sotomayor regained control of the vessel and steered it into what is today called Copano Bay, located in Aransas and Refugio counties. In his search for more protective waters, the captain guided the ship into the Mission River, the stream that emptied into the bay. Aided by strong winds, the barkentine floated swiftly up the rain-swollen river for several miles. As the river narrowed, the current grew stronger and it was with great difficulty that the ship was able to proceed. When a wide tributary to the Mission River with slower moving water loomed ahead, Sotomayor chose to sail into it, hoping his chances would be improved.

It proved to be a mistake. The barkentine had proceeded no more than two or three hundred yards up the tributary when the ship became stuck in the shallow muddy bottom. Efforts to dislodge the ship proved fruitless, and finally Sotomayor instructed his crew to make themselves as comfortable as possible and wait out the rest of the storm.

Two days later when the rain finally ceased, Sotomayor ordered his crew on deck. He discovered he had lost over half of his men to the storm, probably washed overboard by the strong winds and relentless waves. He also noted that the waters of the tributary had receded considerably, leaving most of the hull of the barkentine partially submerged in a sandy shoal. Only an act of God could get the ship off the shoal and back to the gulf.

Realizing his chances of returning to the gulf in the barkentine were gone, Sotomayor and his crewmen simply packed what possessions they could carry, abandoned the stranded vessel, and began the long hike southwestward along the coast toward Mexico, hopeful of reaching a settlement. Only hours from the vessel, Sotomayor and his men were attacked by a party of cannibalistic Karankawa Indians. Defenseless, the entire party was slaughtered in a matter of minutes.

A few miles behind them in the tributary, the tattered canvas sails of the stranded, disabled ship fluttered in the waning coastal breeze. The creaking of the hull could be heard from a long distance as the vessel sank deeper into the mud. Deep inside the hold and lashed to the deck remained the wooden casks holding the uncountable fortune in gold and silver.

Several months later, when Spanish officials learned the fate of their treasure fleet, they assumed that all of the ships had gone down in the storm; thus, a recovery expedition was never organized. They could not have known of the barkentine lost a few short miles inland on a tributary to the Mission River.

During the 1840s, warring Comanches ranged and raided throughout much of Texas from the High Plains to the Gulf Coast. Not only did these fierce Indians seize every opportunity to attack and slay white settlers whom they perceived were intruding into their territory, the Comanches also struck and looted the villages of other tribes, often taking men, women, and children as prisoners to use as slaves.

A party of Comanches was riding toward a Karankawa village located on the coast with the intention of raiding and taking slaves when they chanced upon a peculiar sight. Lying partially buried in a shallow stream were the remains of a sailing ship. For just over twenty years the vessel had lain thus, and the rainy and humid coastal environment had taken its toll. Much of the wooden hull and deck had rotted and was falling apart, and what remained of the three masts had toppled.

A Comanche party such as the one depicted here discovered the wreck
of a Spanish barkentine near Galveston sometime during the 1840s.
Library of Congress

Cautiously, the Indians approached the ship, calling out to it and occasionally firing arrows into the decaying hull. When no response was
forthcoming, the Comanches dismounted, climbed onto the ship, and
explored the mud- and debris-filled vessel. Nothing they encountered
aroused much interest in the Indians until one of them broke open a cask
of gold coins. Though money and wealth in the form of coin were
unimportant to the Comanches, they were smart enough to know that
such things could purchase important arms and ammunition.

After removing the coins from about a half-dozen of the casks and
loading them into saddlebags and pouches, the Comanches were about
to ride away when they were surprised by an approaching band of
Karankawas who initiated an attack. For nearly a half-hour, the Comanches fled in a southwesterly direction across the coastal prairie, the
angry Karankawas close at their heels. Slowed down by the heavy cargo
of gold coins they were transporting, as well as an abundance of goods
taken in earlier raids, the Comanches rode to the top of a low grassy
knoll to make a stand against their attackers. This knoll, according to researchers, lies just north of the city of Refugio.

After dismounting and slashing the throats of several of their horses,
the Comanches took shelter behind the carcasses and fired arrows into
the circling Karankawas. During the skirmish, a few of the Comanches
scraped out a shallow hole in the soft earth of the top of the knoll. Into

the excavation they poured all of the gold coins and covered it up. The Comanches intended to mount up and, once upon their remaining un-encumbered ponies, outrun the attacking Karankawas. At another time, they intended to return to the knoll and retrieve the treasure.

Escaping from their attackers turned out to be more difficult than the Comanches realized. For the next hour the Karankawas effectively pinned down their enemy, lobbing arrows and lances into their midst and killing many. Several more of the mounts were killed by flying arrows, and the rest ran away, leaving the Comanches without a means for es-cape. After capturing the fleeing horses, the Karankawas finally tired of the fight, hurled insults at their defeated enemy, and rode away. When the last of them disappeared over the horizon, the Comanches gathered up what they could carry and, on foot, left the grassy knoll. As far as can be determined, they never returned to the site to recover the fortune in buried gold coins.

Sometime in 1856 or 1857, an elderly crippled Comanche Indian, along with his wife and four children, traveled to the coastal plains area north of Refugio in search of the grassy knoll. The Indian, a member of the party that was attacked by the Karankawas years earlier, spent several weeks in the area searching for the treasure in gold coins he had helped to bury atop the knoll. Unfortunately for him, he was unable to distin-guish the knoll where he and his fellow warriors defended themselves against the Karankawas. As it turns out, there were several knolls in the region, all looking similar.

Having no luck in finding the buried coins, the old Comanche, along with his family, rode back toward the northeast to try to relocate the barkentine. He found it with little difficulty and noted that the ves-sel had sunk even deeper into the soft mud of the stream bottom. When he climbed aboard the rotting ship he saw that the interior was com-pletely filled with mud and sand and most of the deck was covered over as well. Reliving the time he and his fellow warriors first encountered the barkentine, the old Comanche wandered across the vessel, completely unaware that only a few feet below him in the sediment rested millions of dollars worth of treasure in gold and silver.

During the mid-1870s, Anglo settlers began moving into the Texas Gulf Coast area in large numbers. The rich prairie grasses were able to support large herds of cattle and several ranching empires had their ori-gins here during this period. In only a few years, a man named Fagan de-veloped one of the largest and most productive cattle ranches in the re-gion centered near Refugio County.

Since they were located a long distance from forests, Fagan and others who settled in this region often found themselves in need of lumber for the construction of homes, barns, and corrals. Travelers through this area often referred to an old abandoned ship they spotted lying in a tributary of the Mission River, so one day Fagan decided to go investigate for himself and determine if any of the vessel's lumber was worth retrieving.

Following several days of searching, Fagan finally found what was left of the old Spanish barkentine, and he decided some of the old timbers might be suitable for use back at his ranch. One week later, he led several wagonloads of his ranch hands back to the ship where they systematically disassembled portions of it, loaded the wood onto the wagons, and returned to the ranch. As he worked on the ship, rancher Fagan was unaware of the great fortune in gold and silver coins and ingots that lay under his feet.

After salvaging what little usable wood could be found, Fagan abandoned the ship, leaving the rest to continue to decay on the coastal prairie. By 1910, the hot and humid coastal climate, along with the work of termites, rendered the remainder of the ship little more than a mound of rotted debris. The casual traveler through the region during this time could not know that this undistinguished mound in the bed of the stream had once been a proud Spanish barkentine.

The tributary where the ship became mired during the storm of September 1822 became known locally as Barkentine Creek and is described as such on maps today. Somewhere in or near this creek, covered only by a thin layer of prairie soil, lies one of the greatest lost treasures in the history of the United States. There is no way to determine the value of this lost fortune, but experts suggest it may be worth hundreds of millions of dollars.

Occasional searches for the lost treasure of Barkentine Creek have been undertaken, all of which have ended in failure. For the most part, searchers have ranged along the present course of the tributary to the Mission River, swinging metal detectors back and forth in the hope of finding the great deposit of gold and silver coins and ingots.

The probability is great that they are searching in the wrong place. The slow-moving Barkentine Creek, like other such streams with gentle gradients, has meandered much during the almost two centuries since the Spanish vessel became mired in its mud, creating new channels and abandoning old ones. It is quite possible that the remains of the ship, along with the great fortune in buried treasure, lies dozens, if not hundreds, of yards from the present channel.

The wealth of gold coins buried by the Comanche Indians atop the knoll that lies somewhere in the coastal prairie north of the town of Refugio may be only a few inches below the surface and may offer more potential for discovery.

Whoever finds either of these incredible treasures would possess wealth beyond imagining.

II

COLONIAL AMERICA

ROGERS' RANGERS AND
THE LOST SILVER MADONNA

Considered by many to be an important adjunct to the British forces during the Colonial Period was a group of men who served as scouts and mercenaries known as Rogers' Rangers. The Rangers were founded by Robert Rogers, who was born in Methuen, Massachusetts, on November 7, 1731. As a youth, he served as a scout during the conflicts between the settlers and the Indians. From the Indians, Rogers learned stealth, camouflage, and self-sufficiency in the wilderness, skills that were to serve him well throughout his years as the leader of the United States Army's first company of commandos. Rogers and his band of frontiersmen served with the British Army during the French and Indian War (1754–1763) and were responsible for scouting and conducting raids on enemy positions.

Most of the Rangers were farmers and tradesmen from small New England frontier towns. Rogers instructed them in the kind of fighting he learned from the Indians and how to encounter and subdue the enemy under a variety of conditions. He taught them how to track, and how to organize and conduct surprise raids that caught the enemy unaware and unprepared. Though technically soldiers, the Rangers disdained uniforms and authority, and some historians regard them as little more than hired killers. It was also a fact that Rogers allowed his men to loot villages they raided as well as take scalps.

The year 1754 saw the beginning of the French and Indian War. France, its Canadian colonies, and its American Indian allies waged war against Britain and its American colonies. The hostilities started when the French Canadians constructed Fort Duquesne near the present-day city of Pittsburgh, Pennsylvania. The Virginia colony sent out a large force to evict the French Canadians from the territory, which was then claimed by Virginia. The force was led by a twenty-two-year-old lieutenant colonel named George Washington.

Realizing a need for the services provided by Rogers' wilderness-wise and often bloodthirsty fighting force, Major General William Shirley commissioned the Rangers in 1756, awarding Rogers the rank of captain. Initially, it was a group of some sixty men. By mid-1758, Rogers had been promoted to major and given command of nine companies, a total of six hundred men.

During the French and Indian War, relations between the British, the American colonists, and the French Canadians grew extremely tense along the Canadian border, often resulting in minor skirmishes. As confrontations became more frequent and violent, General Jeffrey Amherst, commander of the British troops at Fort Ticonderoga near the New York–Vermont border, was becoming concerned about the growing number of raids launched by the French and their Indian allies. Amherst decided the situation required a retaliative strike, and he sent for Major Rogers.

In truth, Amherst despised Rogers and regarded his charges as undisciplined and insubordinate riff-raff. But he was also smart enough to realize this band of rough-edged, fearless, and skilled fighters was able to accomplish things his own soldiers could not. Amherst believed only Rogers' Rangers could carry out the assignment he had in mind. The commander informed Rogers he wanted him to ride into Canada and launch an attack against an Abenaki Indian village called St. Francis. No prisoners were to be taken, Amherst told Rogers.

Twenty-two days after receiving instruction from Amherst, Rogers and a command of some seven hundred Rangers arrived at the village, thirty on horseback and the rest traveling on foot. Supplies were transported by pack horses. Following brief instructions from Rogers, the Rangers surrounded the sleeping village of St. Francis about four hours before dawn on an October day in 1759. Just as a suggestion of sunlight illuminated the tops of the trees in the encircling forest, Rogers signaled the attack by firing his musket.

As one, the Rangers streamed into the village and began shooting and clubbing the Indians. Many were shot as they slept, others were pulled from their shelters and executed summarily. Women and children were killed indiscriminately, and a Catholic priest was dragged from the rude structure that served as a chapel and shot down.

The raid was such a complete surprise that approximately two hundred Abenakis lay dead about the village after only twenty minutes. Following the brief massacre, the homes were set ablaze and a number of the Rangers roamed among the dead, taking scalps and mutilating the

Robert Rogers, from a 1778 portrait. Library of Congress

corpses. At the same time, another two dozen men entered the chapel and sacked it, taking the golden chalices and candlesticks, silver and gold crosses, and other items.

On reaching the altar, several of the Rangers halted, stunned, and stared in awe at a remarkable statue. It was called the Silver Madonna, and the bright, polished figure reflected the flickering light of the burning village. It is believed that the Silver Madonna, standing just over two feet tall, was crafted from native silver and presented to the Abenaki Indians as a gift.

Following a moment of hesitation, a dozen of the Rangers lifted the heavy object from its pedestal, carried it outside, and tied it to the back of a sturdy pack horse.

After making certain his assignment was carried out and not an Indian remained alive, Rogers quickly reassembled his troops. He told them that a few of the Indians escaped and would no doubt warn others nearby. He said they should expect pursuit at any moment, and it was imperative they begin the long trek back to Fort Ticonderoga immediately.

Invigorated by the bloody battle, the Rangers set out on foot. The officers rode horseback, and the supplies and munitions were transported in the same manner. The last two horses in the retreating file of Rangers carried the loot from the chapel, including the Silver Madonna.

After two hours of hard marching, a rear scout informed Major Rogers that a large force of armed and mounted French soldiers, accompanied by about one hundred Indians, were approaching at a rapid pace. Realizing his men were exhausted from the long march from Fort Ticonderoga, the fight, and the two hours of return march, Rogers knew he needed an advantage. He decided to split his force in an attempt to confuse the pursuers. Rogers himself led half of his Rangers southward toward the colonies, and ordered the remaining half to leave the trail, enter the deep forest, and continue due east for several miles before turning south. The pack horses carrying the Silver Madonna and the church treasures went with the group of men heading east.

Rogers' ploy had no effect whatsoever on the pursuers. When they arrived at the point where the Rangers divided and went their separate ways, the French commanders sent half of their forces to the south and the other half to the east. Knowing they were only a short distance from their quarry, the French, along with their Indian companions, went after the marauders with renewed vigor. Only minutes later, the pursuers overtook both groups of Rangers. Stragglers at the ends of the columns were shot and killed, and the French closed in and engaged the fleeing colonists in hand-to-hand combat. At a huge disadvantage as a result of fatigue and an ill-prepared defense, the Rangers suffered heavy casualties.

The group of Rangers escaping eastward suffered the worst. After two full days of running and fighting, they had had little time to rest and eat, and the French killed about fifty of them. To make matters worse, a severe snowstorm struck the region and caught the Rangers by surprise. Ill-prepared for the freezing temperatures, Rangers began deserting and fleeing southward through the woods at every opportunity.

After finally reaching the southwestern edge of Lake Memphremagog on the Quebec-Vermont border, the pack horse transporting the gold and silver chalices and candlesticks went lame. Rather than risk taking the time to transfer the valuable cargo onto another animal or bury it, the Rangers simply abandoned it. They continued, however, leading the pack horse carrying the Silver Madonna. A short time later, they decided to cross the shallow lake. Once the difficult crossing was made, the party, now reduced in size, proceeded southeastward toward the Connecticut River. The French remained close on their heels, coming near enough to shoot four or five Rangers several times a day. As they pushed on, the party of Rangers continued to be decimated by exhaustion, desertion, and death at the hands of the pursuers.

The contingent of soldiers grew smaller, hungrier, more tired, and more desperate than ever as they plodded through the Vermont woods just yards ahead of the sniping French soldiers. By the time they reached the Connecticut River, the surviving Rangers numbered only four, and they were completely out of food. All they carried were their guns, and one led the pack horse carrying the Silver Madonna.

One of the Rangers, a sergeant by the name of Amos Parsons, was familiar with the region they traveled through. He told his companions he thought he would be able to lead them out of danger. After crossing the Connecticut River and entering New Hampshire near the present-day town of Lancaster, the weary Rangers followed the Israel River upstream and into the foothills of the White Mountains.

By this time, the pursuing French had lost interest and turned back. Parsons led his companions on three more days of slow and difficult hiking through the rugged foothills. Out of food and unsuccessful at finding game, the men were reduced to making soup out of strips of their buckskins. Finally, unable to continue because of starvation and exhaustion, they left the riverbank and ascended a steep trail with several switchbacks and hid themselves in the shelter of an overhanging rock. Here, they untied the Silver Madonna, carried it to a corner of the shelter, and set it upright. Following this, they slaughtered the pack horse, greedily drank the warm blood, and consumed raw flesh they hacked off with their hunting knives. When they were sated, they dropped to the floor of the shelter and slept soundly for the first time in days.

Just before sunrise the following morning, two of the Rangers awoke with severe stomach cramps and Parsons suffered from a fever and delirium. During one of his rages, he spotted the Silver Madonna at the end of the shelter. In his rage, Parsons was convinced the idol was responsible for all of their troubles, for the deaths of his friends, and that there must be a curse associated with it. Maniacally, Parsons grabbed the statue, dragged it to the edge of the shelter floor, and pushed it over, letting it roll down the steep bank, bouncing and sliding over the granite rocks until it plummeted into the Israel River. After watching the Silver Madonna disappear beneath the surging waters of the stream, the deranged Parsons, now screaming and pulling clumps of matted hair from his head, raced down the trail and into the woods, never to be seen again.

For another two days and nights, the three surviving Rangers remained in the rock shelter trying to recover from their exhaustion and sickness. On the third morning, one of them awoke to find his companions dead. Weak and confused, he fled the shelter and resumed hiking upstream along the trail that paralleled the Israel River. He hiked all day, then took shelter in a hollow log for the night. The next morning, he resumed his journey, hoping and praying he would encounter someone who might offer help. After about two hours of walking, he arrived at a small settlement of woodcutters, some four or five families. On seeing the pathetic, emaciated wretch wearing clothes that were little more than tatters, the settlers took him in, fed him, and tried to make him comfortable.

Days passed as the Ranger gradually regained his health. He was lucid for short periods, but often awoke from his slumber screaming and delirious. As he was being ministered to, the Ranger told his caregivers the story of the raid on the Abenaki village, the theft of the Silver Madonna, and the ordeal of fleeing from the French soldiers and the Indians through the wilderness. In remarkable detail, he related how he lay in sickness in the rock shelter and watched Sergeant Parsons seize the holy icon, drag it to the edge of the bank, and push it over and into the Israel River.

Though the Ranger regained most of his heath, his mind never fully recovered from the experience. During the second month of living among the woodcutters, he went completely insane.

Several weeks after listening to the story of the Silver Madonna, four of the woodcutters followed the trail along the Israel River until they came to the rock shelter described by the Ranger. They climbed the steep path to the shelter and inside they found the decayed remains of two men and a horse. They walked along the river bank searching for some sign of the Silver Madonna in the water, but it was too deep and roiling for them to detect anything. They returned to the settlement empty-handed.

As far as anyone knows, the Silver Madonna has never been recovered, and most researchers are convinced it still lies in the mud and gravel of the Israel River somewhere below the rock shelter. Considering the great weight and specific gravity of the statue, it is unlikely that it traveled downstream with the current very far from the point where it entered the river. Given the texture of the river bottom in this region, there is reason to believe that the heavy object sank into the mud, perhaps several inches below the bed of the stream. The point along the Israel River has been determined to lie somewhere just downstream from the small town of Jefferson.

Major Robert Rogers and a number of his men survived the flight from the French soldiers and went on to participate in other battles. In 1760, Rogers' Rangers played an important role in the capture of Montreal.

The French and Indian War, which was also the prelude to the Seven Years' War between the British and French and their allies in Europe, was ended with the Treaty of Paris in 1763. In 1765, Rogers traveled to England. There, he wrote two books: *Journals* and *A Concise Account of North America*. A short time later, he was given command of Fort Michilimackinac in what is now the state of Michigan. He was relieved soon afterward and he made another trip to England. In 1775, he returned to Revolutionary America but remained loyal to the British. In 1776, he formed the Queen's American Rangers but recorded not a single noteworthy achievement. He returned again to England in 1780. Robert Rogers died in London on May 18, 1795.

To this day, the Silver Madonna remains one of the most cherished lost artifacts from the French and Indian War. If recovered, its value to collectors is estimated to well over one million dollars.

BENEDICT ARNOLD'S LOST REVOLUTIONARY WAR TREASURE

Most Americans link the name Benedict Arnold with treason. In fact, the very name has become synonymous with disloyalty as a result of Arnold's betrayal to the United States when he aligned himself with the British during the Revolutionary War. Few, however, are aware that this historic individual, once a trusted general in George Washington's army, was closely associated with a wooden chest filled with gold coins that was lost deep in the Maine wilderness during a forced march in 1775.

Arnold was born in 1741 in Norwich, Connecticut. As a youth he was apprenticed to a pharmacist and became a student of the science. Years later as a young man, he owned and operated a pharmacy and a bookstore in New Haven, and in time grew wealthy.

In 1774, Arnold became a captain in the Connecticut militia. In 1775 when the Americans decided it was time to fight for their independence from British rule, the Revolutionary War got under way, a war that led to the birth of the United States of America. Benedict Arnold was commissioned as a colonel and soon drew the attention of military commander General George Washington. On May 10, Arnold, along with Ethan Allen, led eighty-three troopers in the attack and capture of Fort Ticonderoga.

George Washington began to regard Arnold as one of his most competent and trusted officers and often sought his help in various campaigns. Close to the onset of the war, Colonel Arnold submitted to Washington a carefully thought-out strategy for the invasion and capture of Quebec City in the Canadian province of Quebec. Washington was aware of Arnold's familiarity with the site as a result of previous expeditions to the region. He offered Arnold the responsibility of leading a campaign through the wilderness of Maine, across the international border, into the Canadian province of Quebec, and directly to the perimeter of the walled fortress in the city from where he would launch an attack.

Because Colonel Arnold required significant funds to employ guides, and purchase equipment, supplies, and ammunition, as well as pay his troops, Washington consigned to him a medium-sized wooden chest containing $54,000 worth of gold coins.

The soldiers, 1,100 of them, were loaded onto ships that sailed out of Boston Harbor on September 13, 1775. A short time later, the vessels docked at Newburyport, Massachusetts, some sixty sea miles to the north, where they took on supplies, barrels of fresh water, and more troops, then set sail once again. Three weeks later, during the first week of October, the ships anchored at the mouth of the Kennebec River near the present-day town of Brunswick, Maine. Here, Arnold intended to transfer soldiers and supplies to rafts, pole up the river as far as they could go, then strike out through the Maine forests on foot toward Canada.

Earlier, Arnold arranged for the purchase of a number of log rafts, which were awaiting him and his troops at a nearby settlement. On inspection, however, the colonel discovered most of them to be rotten and unserviceable. Arnold immediately hired several local woodsmen and carpenters and commissioned a fleet of brand new rafts suitable for transporting the soldiers, the heavy cannons, and all of the supplies. Arnold was disturbed by the delay and irritated at the inconvenience. He was also annoyed at the expense. Arnold was forced to remove some of the money from the chest to pay for the work. As he did so, about one dozen soldiers standing nearby gazed at the immense fortune in gold coins lying within.

Days passed while the new rafts were being completed and Arnold fumed at the prolonged delay. He was concerned that his company of soldiers would arrive at Quebec City far past the time when they would be able to launch an effective assault. When at last the rafts were ready, Arnold had them loaded at once and he and his men set out upstream. Trying to make up the time that was lost, Arnold forced his soldiers into long days of difficult travel.

Poling the large, heavily laden rafts upstream was demanding, tedious labor, and occasionally the soldiers were forced to attach lines to the clumsy vessels, wade to the shore, and pull the crafts over sand bars, submerged logs, and other obstacles. Autumn storms drenched the troops with heavy rains, blowing wind, and cold.

The forced expedition, aggravated by the obsessive, demanding Arnold, suffered one disaster after another. Shallow, muddy swamps slowed travel. Portaging the heavy rafts, packs of supplies, and cannons around the oft-occurring rapids and waterfalls sometimes took days. A number of cannons as well as packs containing supplies and food were lost when the leather straps securing them to the rafts parted, causing them to topple into the surging river.

As a result of so many of the stores being swept away, food shortages grew acute, and meals were cancelled, all adding to the plummeting morale of the soldiers. In an attempt to remedy the situation, Arnold sent sharpshooters out into the woods to find game. Several became lost and never returned, and it is believed they simply deserted while they had the chance. Regardless, little game was to be found and the hunger problems only increased.

Benedict Arnold. Library of Congress

By the end of the second week of traveling on the river, the troops were reduced to making soups out of their boot leather. Many were emaciated, weak, and suffering from dysentery. An early freeze only made matters worse. With the likelihood of facing greater hardships, more and more soldiers deserted.

At some point along the journey, the rafts left the Kennebec River and were poled for some distance up a tributary. At another point, rafts and equipment were carried from one river channel across a ridge to that of another. This represented even more aggravating delay.

Late one afternoon, the raft carrying Arnold's chest of coins was caught in a tricky series of rapids. The stress of the strong current snapped the weakened lashing and several of the logs separated, causing the heavy gold-filled chest to plunge into the icy torrent. According to one account, the event occurred on the Dead River a few miles north of the present-day community of Eustis.

Arnold was devastated by the loss of the chest and the money that had been designated to finance the expedition. Realizing he possessed neither the time nor the equipment necessary to retrieve the chest from the deep, frigid waters, he could do little more than urge his remaining soldiers forward and try to reach Quebec City in time to launch an effective attack.

Arnold's diminished force finally arrived at the south bank of the St. Lawrence River across from Quebec City on December 13. Too exhausted and undersupplied to strike the enemy, they established a camp and awaited developments. Earlier, on November 12, General Richard Montgomery took Montreal, the capital of Quebec Province. He then ordered his troops to move one hundred sixty miles northeast to Quebec City where they were to join forces with Arnold's command. On December 31, the combined forces attacked Quebec City in a blinding snowstorm. At the end of the fierce battle, the British prevailed and the Americans suffered an embarrassing defeat. Montgomery was dead, and Arnold was incapacitated as a result of a serious wound to his right knee. Despite this setback, Arnold organized and maintained a tight blockade around Quebec City throughout the winter.

Though a failure in many respects, Arnold's expedition through the Maine wilderness is regarded as one of the classic marches in military history. When Colonel Arnold was finally able to travel, he returned to General Washington's command where he reported his misfortunes. No attempt was ever made to return to the location where the chest of gold coins had spilled into the river.

For the courage he exhibited during the march and the subsequent fight at Quebec City, Benedict Arnold was promoted to brigadier general in 1776. In October of that same year, he distinguished himself once again in the Battle of Valour Island, a naval conflict on Lake Champlain.

In 1779, Arnold was called upon to account for the loss of the $54,000 in gold coins entrusted to him. It is because of his formal testimony, as well as that of others, at this hearing that history is aware of the circumstances.

In February 1777, Arnold was eligible for promotion to major general. In spite of the fact that he had seniority over the five others who were granted the rank, he was ignored. The seeds of bitterness against his military peers and the structure of the new government were sown.

In May, General Washington effected Arnold's promotion to major general as a reward for his bravery during the expulsion of a British raiding party from Connecticut. In 1778, Arnold was given command of Philadelphia. Unfortunately, he proved to be a poor administrator, was suspected of misappropriating funds and manpower, and endured heavy criticism from his peers. He was eventually court-martialed. Ultimately, Arnold was formally cleared of all the charges but received a severe reprimand. His bitterness grew.

Arnold began to believe his country was ungrateful for all of the service and sacrifice he had devoted to it. More, he believed it unjust in its treatment of him. As a result, he quietly solicited a relationship with the enemy, the British. With their assistance, he instigated a plan to surrender an important military base, West Point, to British Army commander Sir Henry Clinton. After carefully outlining his strategy, Arnold had it forwarded to Clinton by courier. The courier, however, was captured, and Arnold's treachery discovered. He fled immediately to New York City where he became a brigadier general in the British Army.

His troubles were not over. Arnold demanded a payment of twenty thousand pounds from the British for losses he incurred as a result of his efforts to join them, but they paid him only a bit over six thousand. Although disheartened, Arnold led British forces on successful raids on Richmond, Virginia, and New London, Connecticut, destroying both cities.

After the war, Arnold left America for England in 1782. There, he was greeted warmly by King George III, but scorned by the citizenry. Though his duplicity may have aided the British in some ways, he was still a traitor, a fact not lost on the common man.

Arnold spent his remaining years as a merchant involved in the growing West Indies trade. Burdened with debt, discouraged that he never received the honor he believed he deserved, and glum over the fact that no one ever seemed to trust him, he died on June 14, 1801.

A few researchers contend that Benedict Arnold did not lose the gold entrusted to him at all, but secretly cached it somewhere along the route traveled. He intended, his critics say, to return and retrieve it at a later date. What this presumption is based on is not known for certain, but some suggest that Arnold's subsequent reputation as a traitor made him a suspect in the eyes of a few. The truth is, numerous eyewitnesses who testified at the inquisition stated that the chest did indeed slip from its position on the raft, was lost in the current, and never seen after the disaster on the Dead River. It has also been argued that Arnold may have removed the coins from the chest well before the incident.

If Arnold was telling the truth, and there is no compelling reason to suspect he wasn't, then there is a great likelihood that the chest, perhaps still intact and filled with a fortune in gold coins, may be lying at the bottom of that stream today. Experts suggest the cold water would be helpful in preserving the wooden chest. Gold coins worth in the neighborhood of $54,000 in 1775 would be worth millions today, both in real and antique value.

Some who are convinced Benedict Arnold's chest of gold coins still lies near a set of rapids on the Dead River are also convinced it is retrievable. Interest in this historically significant treasure remains high among some, and in recent years Arnold's testimony has been researched several times. Professional treasure hunters armed with sensitive gold-detecting devices have made forays into the wilderness area of the Dead River in the hope of locating and recovering the fortune.

At this writing, they are still searching.

LOST GOLD PAYROLL

The French and Indian War, 1754–1763, provided the setting for a number of famous battles and proved formative in the careers of several military and political leaders, George Washington among the most prominent.

Another principal figure during the war was Edward Braddock, the British-appointed commander-in-chief of the colonies. Braddock was born in Scotland. Attracted to military service, he joined the Second Guards in 1710 and consistently rose through the ranks as a result of distinguished service in a number of British campaigns.

History books tell us that the French and Indian Wars began as a result of the French constructing Fort Duquesne on the banks of the Ohio River in Pittsburgh, Pennsylvania. Perceived as an intrusion into British possessions, the colonial army retaliated, thus initiating the hostilities that were to last for nine years.

Perceiving a need for his special brand of leadership, the Crown sent Braddock to the Americas to help in the fight. He arrived in Virginia in 1755 with two regiments and was appalled at finding the colonies without significant troops or resources, and practically devoid of organization and leadership. He lost no time in training new recruits and distinguishing himself in several encounters with the enemy.

Fort Duquesne remained one of the principal French strongholds and Braddock determined that the best way to rid the region of the French was to attack the fort and drive them from it. With his two regiments of well over 1,500 men, along with artillery and supplies, even a payroll wagon along with the paymaster, Braddock led his men from Fort Cumberland, Maryland, some 220 miles across the Alleghenies, a journey over bad roads with poor horses. He finally arrived at a point about eight miles from Fort Duquesne where, on July 9, he was about to give the order to set up camp when he was attacked by a French force of nine hundred.

Braddock had overestimated his ability to sneak up to the fort undetected and underestimated the abilities of the French and their Canadian and Indian allies. The French force was scattered and hidden throughout the adjacent forest while the British soldiers, in the manner of British military tactics, were clustered together and wearing red uniforms, presenting an easy target for the enemy marksmen.

So surprised by the attack were the British soldiers, and so completely unprepared to defend themselves, that they scurried away in a disorderly retreat. Braddock was wounded early in the battle and died four days later. The retreat became a rout, and after running for a few miles, they were set upon by yet another contingent of French soldiers coming from another direction. The subsequent battle lasted for nearly three hours. Over half of the outnumbered, outgunned, and outsmarted British were killed or wounded, and the survivors, knowing they would be slain if they remained in the area, fled deeper into the Pennsylvania woods, a flight known as "Braddock's Retreat."

When it was clear the French and Indian forces would overpower the British, the paymaster assigned six soldiers to pack the payroll, all in gold coins, onto the fastest, stoutest horses they could acquire and deliver it back to Fort Cumberland in western Maryland with all possible haste. The estimated value of the payroll in 1755 was $25,000. The six mounted troopers departed with four payroll-laden horses and, delighted with the opportunity to leave the scene of battle, made their way in a southeasterly direction through the woods.

Delivering the gold payroll to Fort Cumberland was not to be as easy as the soldiers anticipated. During the first several days of their flight, they suffered ambushes by French soldiers, each time barely escaping with their lives. At times, they encountered scouting patrols and were forced to leave the trail and hide among the trees and rocks until it was safe to continue.

On at least two occasions, the payroll guards were overtaken from behind by French troops and pursued for miles. During one such chase, two of the guards were wounded by gunfire. Because they were unfamiliar with the woods and were traveling roads unknown to them, the six soldiers often became lost. Additional skirmishes with the French and their Indian allies forced them farther and farther from the main routes and miles from the road to Fort Cumberland. One afternoon, they chanced upon an old military road they recognized and they calculated the fort was still forty miles west of their location.

Tired and hungry, the guards and their weary horses plodded onward until they believed they were only about fifteen miles from the fort. At one point along the road they decided to rest themselves and the animals. The ranking guard pointed to a low area just off the trail that appeared to be a suitable location for a respite. Here there was a small pool of water and lush grasses where the horses could drink and graze for a while. As the soldiers rode toward the location, they were set upon once again by French soldiers who were lying in ambush. Two of the guards were killed with the first volley.

During the next hour as the four remaining soldiers, leading the payroll-packed horses, fled from the pursuing French, two more were shot from their saddles and killed. The two survivors decided to seek cover and make a stand, and they reined their mounts toward a cluster of rocks. Here, they fired upon their pursuers, eventually driving them away. Not wishing to continue herding the extra horses, the two soldiers repacked the bags of gold coins onto their own mounts, turned the rest loose, and continued on their way.

The dramatically increased weight of the packs of gold on the mounts soon began taking its toll. The animals tired rapidly, slowing to a hoof-dragging walk in only a few minutes. Sensing that the animals were unable to endure much more, the two soldiers decided to unload the gold, hide it somewhere, and return for it with a platoon of armed and mounted troops after reaching Fort Cumberland.

The road the soldiers traveled paralleled a small stream. Near a place where the water flowed around a large boulder in the middle of the channel, one of the riders spotted a shallow cave in a hill on the north side of the trail. He pointed it out to his companion, and together the two rode toward it, forcing their tired horses up the steep incline. When they reached the low cave, they pulled the heavy packs from the mounts and stacked them inside, covering them with brush, rock, soil, and leaves. This done, the two remounted, and rode back down the slope and away toward the fort.

They had not been on the trail for more than ten minutes when they were ambushed once again, this time by three Indians. One of the soldiers was killed instantly from a bullet fired from an Indian's musket. The remaining guard was also struck and knocked from his horse. On hitting the ground, he quickly crawled away into the thick brush and managed to elude the attackers. Dazed and weak from loss of blood, the last guard, living on edible roots and berries, was found along the military road ten days later by a British scouting patrol. After he was transported to Fort Cumberland and treated by the post physician, the guard provided details of the attack on Braddock's command by the French and Indians, the subsequent escape with the payroll, the difficulties encountered in carrying out the assignment, and the caching of the gold coins in the small cave near the stream.

Two weeks later when the guard had recovered and was able to travel, he led a platoon of soldiers back to the area where he believed the cave was located. When he arrived at the place where he was convinced he and his companion had hidden the gold, he became confused, was unable to find the portion of the stream containing the large boulder, and confessed he was lost. Several caves were found among the rocks in the side of the hill adjacent to the stream, but none of them contained the payroll.

After three days of searching and not finding anything, the platoon sergeant ordered the contingent back to Fort Cumberland. Several members of the platoon, along with some officers stationed at the fort, were convinced the guard hid the money and intended to keep it for himself. Others of a more sympathetic nature believed that, as a result of being wounded and living in terror and hiding for over a week, the guard was simply confused and could not remember landmarks. Still others thought he had gone insane.

Several additional forays into the region in search of the missing gold payroll ended in failure, and the British officials finally gave up.

In 1881, a deer hunter stumbled across some scattered and weathered human bones in the woods not far from the tiny Maryland community of Piney Grove, less than twenty miles east of Cumberland. Among the old bones were a few rusted buttons which were later identified as the type used on uniforms worn by British soldiers during the French and Indian War.

Several researchers familiar with the tale of the lost British payroll hypothesized that the bones may have belonged to the guard who was killed shortly after the caching of the gold. Weeks later, a handful of men who were convinced they could find the payroll enlisted the hunter to lead them back to the region where he found the bones. Though an attempt was made, the hunter was unable to remember the exact location and the expedition ended in failure.

In 1907, a woodsman who earned a spare living trapping for furs in the Maryland panhandle and southern Pennsylvania took shelter in a small cave one afternoon during a severe rainstorm. As he waited for the rains to abate, he gathered together a pile of branches and leaves from the floor of the cave with which to start a small fire for warmth. In the process, he discovered several pieces of rotted leather under the debris, the kind that might have come from a saddlebag or a stout pouch. More concerned about his comfort than anything else, the woodsman kindled a blaze and warmed himself until the rain finally stopped. Thinking no more about the pieces of leather on the floor of the cave, he left.

Nearly a decade passed when the woodsman chanced to mention the incident to a friend who was intimate with the tale of the lost British Army payroll. Believing he may have stumbled onto the cache years earlier, the woodsman made several attempts to relocate it but was never successful.

October of 1941 saw more rain than normal. Following a three-day storm, a Piney Grove resident was out for a hike along the old military road that led to old Fort Cumberland when he spotted something shining in the road just ahead. On investigating, he discovered a gold British coin. Casting about for other such riches, the hiker noted several small rivulets flowing down an adjacent slope, thin, narrow streams of runoff coming from higher up the hill. Believing the coin might have washed down onto the trail from a higher level, he climbed a few steps up the slope and was quickly rewarded with the discovery of yet another coin. A few more paces uphill, and the soft soil of the slope yielded to a rocky outcrop. Though he searched for another two hours, the hiker found no more coins.

Eight months later the hiker learned the story of the lost British payroll, and that it had been cached in a small cave close to where he had been hiking that day. Determined to find the cache, the hiker returned to the area where he found the coins. It was the middle of June when he arrived, and the slope of the hillside was covered in summer grasses, causing the environment to appear quite different from how it looked the previous October. Though he came to the region several times over the next two months, he was never able to find anything. He returned the following October and another heavy rainstorm had drenched the area, but he had no success.

General Edward Braddock's lost payroll of gold coins has intrigued researchers for over two centuries. Many who have invested considerable time in studying the details of the tales place the location of the hidden

coins somewhere a bit less than twenty miles east of Cumberland, Maryland, and not far from the old military road. While most of the available
documentation strongly argues for this location, others are convinced the
payroll never made it that far and feel they have reason to believe the
gold was hidden just across the border in Pennsylvania.

A coin collector who was invited to provide an estimate of today's
value of the 1775 British gold coins suggested that, if found, they would
bring well over one million dollars, perhaps much more when the historical and antique value is considered.

Based on the evidence, the gold British coins still lie on the floor of
the remote, hard-to-find cave near a small stream not far from the old
military road. Today, they are likely covered by a layer of soil and other
debris and mixed with what remains of the pieces of rotted leather that
once comprised the pouches in which they were carried.

THE LOST TREASURE OF THE
MARQUIS DE LAFAYETTE

Born Marie Joseph Paul Yves Roche Gilbert du Montier of the French aristocracy, the Marquis de Lafayette became an important figure during the American Revolution. He was born in France in 1757 to wealthy parents. His father died in battle when Lafayette was a boy, and his mother passed away eleven years later, leaving him the family fortune. He studied at a French military academy in Versailles, married the sixteen-year-old daughter of an influential family, and was promoted to the rank of captain in the cavalry.

Impressed with and fascinated by the ideals and objectives of the American colonials, Lafayette traveled to America at the age of twenty to join the rebellion. Here, he believed, was an opportunity for him to fight against the British and achieve military glory. He bought a ship, loaded it with provisions and arms, and, with a company of soldiers that he recruited himself, departed for the American colonies.

Not long after arriving in the colonies, Lafayette became acquainted with General George Washington. The Frenchman admired and respected the Revolutionary War commander's leadership and courage. Washington, in turn, was impressed with the idealistic Frenchman who believed strongly in the colonial ideals. The two men forged a strong bond, and in a relatively short time Lafayette was elevated to the rank of major general in the colonial army.

Lafayette was wounded at the Battle of Brandywine, where he was victorious. His bravery earned him command of an entire division of soldiers. Later, he served with Washington at Valley Forge during the terrible winter of 1777–1778.

Lafayette worked tirelessly trying to secure funding for the American war effort from the French government. By 1778, the colonials were running short of arms, ammunition, and supplies and were desperately seeking support wherever they could find it. The French political leaders, however, were hesitant to become involved in American affairs because they feared British reprisal, and they denied Lafayette's request for funding.

Undaunted, Lafayette turned to a number of prominent French businessmen already known to be in support of colonial ideals and who, at one time or another, had provided secret funding. On the condition that they remain anonymous, the businessmen agreed to raise and donate money and supplies and have them shipped to the colonies.

The sum of fifty thousand dollars in gold coins and bullion was accumulated from a number of Europeans sympathetic to the American cause, along with a significant amount of supplies and ammunition, and secretly loaded aboard several French merchant vessels. When all was ready, the fleet sailed for the French West Indies in the Caribbean Sea where the gold, ammunition, and supplies were transferred to the French frigate *Dupre*. The *Dupre* was owned by Jean-Pierre Clement, a notorious pirate and friend of Lafayette. Clement saw an opening in the growing business opportunities to be found in America and was only too happy to be involved.

In July 1778, the *Dupre*, loaded with the necessary goods and the gold, set sail from the West Indies to America, its destination a small island off the coast of Virginia. Though French merchant ships were commonly seen in Atlantic waters during this time, the British, ever on the alert for the increase in the smuggling of essential war goods to the Americans, were under orders to fire upon any vessel that appeared suspicious.

After steering a course far to the north of the British-held Bahama Islands, the *Dupre* headed for the east coast of America and eventually arrived just off the shores of North Carolina. Watchful of British warships, Clement steered the *Dupre* northward along the coastline toward Smith Island, the predetermined location off the coast of Virginia. Smith Island was one of the southernmost islets associated with the long, narrow peninsula that separated the Atlantic Ocean from the Chesapeake Bay.

Months earlier, Lafayette made arrangements for the *Dupre* to drop anchor about one hundred yards off Smith Island on the Atlantic side sometime during mid-August. Here, the cargo of gold and supplies was to be transferred into longboats and then delivered to the appropriate colonial leaders at some unnamed Virginia location. Lafayette, along with twelve hand-picked men, had earlier rowed out to Smith Island to await the arrival of the French vessel.

The mid-August heat and humidity was almost unbearable for the thirteen men hiding in a thick grove of trees on Smith Island. For days they waited for the *Dupre*, and it was with considerable relief that the French vessel was finally spotted one day around midmorning approaching the island from the south. The men walked out to the beach to signal the ship.

At the same time, one of the soldiers spotted a British flotilla consisting of six warships rounding the northern end of the island and coming fast, all bearing down on the *Dupre*. The Americans tried in vain to warn the French ship, and then for their own safety retreated to the cover of trees on the island.

The attention of Clement and his crew aboard the *Dupre* was focused on the lowering of the mainsail and dropping anchor, and they did not see the oncoming warships. When the attacking fleet was finally spotted by one of the *Dupre*'s crewmen, it was too late to prepare for battle. With the mainsail down, escape was impossible, so Clement attempted to rally his men to a spirited defense of the ship.

The effort was in vain. The *Dupre*, lying still in the calm, open waters just off Smith Island, was no match for the British warships, all highly maneuverable, fast, well-armed, and staffed with experienced officers, seamen, and soldiers. As soon as the flotilla was within range of the

Lafayette (right) with George Washington at Valley Forge. Library of Congress

Dupre, the ships opened fire, attacking ferociously and mercilessly with a deafening bombardment from dozens of cannons. Their clear intention was to send the frigate to the bottom of the sea.

Helpless, Lafayette and his men could do little but watch the disaster from the concealment of the trees on Smith Island. Shattered and splintered from the ceaseless cannon fire, the *Dupre* listed helplessly to one side for a few minutes, then sank beneath the waves, carrying the cargo of gold and silver bullion, coins, ammunition, and supplies with it.

Lafayette and his charges remained in hiding on the island until the British warships sailed away. Not equipped for recovering the sunken gold, he loaded his men into the rowboats the following morning and proceeded to the rendezvous point somewhere on the southeast Virginia coast. Humbled and bowed, Lafayette was forced to report his failure.

Though his plan to acquire French funding for the American war effort did not work out, Lafayette went on to distinguish himself in a number of other ways throughout the remainder of the American Revolution. Additional attempts to secure funding from French businessmen were successful, and it was in some part due to these contributions that the war was successfully waged.

Lafayette returned to France in 1782 and was given the rank of brigadier general in the French army. He was named commander of the French National Guard, becoming one of the most powerful men in that country. Falling into disfavor with the French king and queen, Lafayette was branded a traitor and fled to Austria. There, he was imprisoned for five years. He died in France in 1834.

Because the close attention of the Revolutionary War leaders was, of necessity, focused on the struggle, no immediate attempts were made to retrieve the gold and silver coins and bullion lying a short distance offshore from Smith Island. As time passed, and the demands on military and political leaders remained high, the matter of the *Dupre* and its precious cargo was soon forgotten.

Today, no record exists of an organized attempt to recover the lost gold of the *Dupre*. In fact, no one is entirely certain of the exact location of the sunken vessel just east of Virginia's Smith Island. The subject has been debated for the past century, with some claiming the ship went down near the southern end of the island while others insist it came to rest on the sea floor closer to the northern shore.

The $50,000 in gold coins and bullion would command a real and antique value of several million dollars today. It is probable that most of the remains of the *Dupre* have rotted away during the past two centuries it has lain on the sandy continental shelf of the Atlantic Ocean near Smith Island. The gold, however, although likely encrusted with sea life and ocean debris, is undoubtedly still lying on the bottom.

There is a definite possibility that Atlantic storms have been responsible for carrying some of the remains of the *Dupre* from its resting place on the ocean floor to the sandy shore of Smith Island. Over the years, fishermen and explorers have reported finding artifacts from what is clearly a French vessel washed up on shore following storms. Interest in the *Dupre* and its shipment of gold was rekindled in 1991 when a beachcomber found a French gold coin with a 1777 mint date washed up on the western shore of the island following a storm.

THE GEORGE WASHINGTON
DOLLARS

Around midnight one moonless night in 1779 during the Revolutionary War, several wooden chests containing specially minted gold coins were stolen from the Continental Army at the small Connecticut village of East Granby and a short time later buried on the bank of the East Fork of nearby Salmon Brook. The actual value of this shipment of gold coins has been debated for more than two centuries, but most experts have concluded it was worth approximately $2.5 million in 1779. Save for a few of the coins, they have never been recovered.

During the 1770s, Lemuel Bates served in the Continental Army, eventually attaining the rank of captain. At the same time, he owned a tavern located less than a mile north of East Granby. The tavern, along a well-traveled route that ran from Philadelphia to Boston, served meals and liquors and also rented rooms. Members of the Revolutionary Army often used Bates' Tavern as a meeting place.

Just past sundown one evening in 1779, Bates, who was tending bar, heard the sound of a large caravan arriving outside the tavern. Stepping out the front door, he observed thirteen wagons, each pulled by a team of four horses and all accompanied by a large contingent of soldiers, pull to the rear of the tavern and form a tight circle. Moments later, the Revolutionary commander of the party climbed down off the lead wagon and approached the tavern owner. He explained that the caravan had left Boston several days earlier and was bound for Philadelphia, some two hundred miles by wagon road to the southwest. He told Bates the travel was slow because of the heavy cargo they were transporting. Pointing toward the wagons, the commander explained to Bates that each was piled high with wooden trunks and chests filled with gold coins, all of them specially minted dollars and each bearing the likeness of George Washington. The coins, referred to as "Washington dollars," were minted in France and represented a loan to the struggling Continental Congress from the French government. Other wooden trunks on the wagons contained supplies and ammunition.

While the commander visited with Bates on the front porch of the tavern, several of the curious East Granby townsfolk arrived to examine the circled wagons. Rarely did such a large wagon train pass through this region, and the citizens stared in wonder at it and the soldiers who accompanied it. As more and more of them gathered, they ventured into the circle of wagons. All at once, about two dozen soldiers, all dressed in the uniforms of the Continental Army, brandished weapons and warned the citizens away with threats of death.

After negotiating terms for meals and lodging for his troopers, the commander returned to the wagons and posted several armed guards about the perimeter to watch over the vehicles and their contents.

During the next few hours, word of the wagon train spread quickly throughout the region. In a short time, a contingent of Tories—Americans sympathetic to the British—gathered in secret at the home of a local official. They discussed the cargo of gold in the wagons and made plans to seize it.

Another two hours passed, and the Tories, under cover of night, crept toward the guarded wagon train and concealed themselves among the nearby trees and brush. When their leaders were convinced most of the soldiers were sound asleep in the tavern, they voiced a low signal, slipped up on the guards, and slit their throats, killing them all. Quietly, they hitched the horses back up to the wagons and drove them away toward the west and into the night.

Shortly after dawn, several early rising soldiers walked to the rear of the tavern and discovered the wagons gone and their companions dead. They alerted the commander, and a search was immediately organized. With some of the soldiers on borrowed horses and most of them afoot, they followed the clear, winding trail left by the wagons through the woods.

About two hours later, the wagons and teams were found in a farmer's pasture less than two miles from Bates' Tavern. From the condition of the horses, it was apparent they had been driven a considerable distance and returned to this location. When the wagons were inspected, it was discovered that every chest containing the Washington dollars was missing. When the farmer was questioned, he professed surprise at learning the wagons and horses were on his land. In spite of his denial, the commander ordered his house, barn, and outbuildings searched, all to no avail. For nearly a week, the Continental soldiers remained in the area searching houses and barns but found nothing. With little choice, the soldiers returned to Boston to report the loss of the shipment of gold coins and await their fate.

One hundred one years after the theft of the shipment of Washington dollars, a resident of Hartford County, in which East Granby is located, wrote a book about the region's history and related the story of the theft of the Washington dollars from Bates' Tavern during the middle of the night in 1779.

In one chapter, the author, Richard H. Phelps, told an incredible story of a man named Henry Wooster. Wooster, a resident of East Granby during the 1770s, was constantly in trouble with the law. He was also a Tory.

About five months after the theft of the Washington dollars, Wooster was convicted of stealing a cow from one of his neighbors and sentenced to hard labor at Newgate Prison, located just outside the town of East Granby. After serving just over six months, Wooster escaped from the prison and made his way on foot to the coast. Here, he obtained work on a freighter leaving for England. Weeks later, after arriving in London, he collected his pay and decided to take up residence and become a model citizen.

Several months after Wooster arrived in England, his mother, who still lived in East Granby, received a letter from him wherein he confessed his part in the theft of the chests filled with Washington dollars from the Continental Army caravan parked behind Bates' Tavern.

According to Wooster's letter, the entire wagon train had been taken and driven from the tavern by a band of Tories. A few hours before dawn, they arrived at a location somewhere along the east bank of the East Fork of Salmon Brook. Here, the coins, still in the wooden chests, were buried close to the stream. The group of Tories made an agreement among themselves that they would return at some later date, exhume the gold, and use it to help the British in the war effort. Each man swore he would honor the agreement under penalty of death.

As the Tories completed the task of filling the large hole and covering the treasure, dawn broke over the forest to the east. Finished, the Tories climbed aboard the wagons and headed back toward East Granby by a different route. On reaching a large pasture less than an hour later, they abandoned the wagons and teams and returned to their homes.

About six weeks following the theft of the coins, the Tories met secretly in the woods at a remote location far from town in order to make a determination relative to the Washington dollars. As they were discussing alternatives, they were attacked by a band of Indians. Surprised and underarmed, all were killed but Wooster, who managed to sneak away in the darkness.

With all of his companions dead, Wooster began making plans to return to the site where the gold coins were buried and retrieve them for himself. As he made his plans and dreamed of what he would do with his newfound wealth, Wooster was caught stealing his neighbor's cow, tried, convicted, and sent to prison. At the first opportunity, he escaped and fled to England.

Though he often thought about the gold and was tempted to return from England to recover it, he was never able to do so. In the letter to his mother, Wooster provided no directions to the treasure site, only stating that it was located on the east bank of the East Fork of Salmon Brook. Though many believe Wooster's mother begged him for more information about the location of the buried Washington dollars in a subsequent letter, he died in England without revealing any pertinent information whatsoever.

Though dozens of East Granby residents searched for the Washington dollars during the months after it was stolen, none were successful, and as the decades passed the event was largely forgotten.

Until 1944.

During that year, Hartford County experienced several days of heavy rains and flooding. River channels overflowed, and the high-velocity currents eroded away stream banks, sometimes causing large trees to topple into the water and float downstream. Two days after the torrential downpours when the stream flow had returned to near-normal, an East Granby resident was hiking along the bank of the East Fork of Salmon Brook when he spied something glinting at the bottom of the stream. Wading into the river, he retrieved the object that caught his attention—it was a gold Washington dollar.

After the man related his discovery in town, a number of citizens who knew the tale of the buried Tory treasure rushed to the stream to look for more of the coins. Though the search continued for several days, no more coins were found.

In 1958, three teenage boys were playing along the bank of the East Fork of Salmon Brook when they discovered three strange coins. A week later, one of the boys showed the coins to his father who, after consulting several rare coin catalogs and a collector in Hartford, identified them as Washington dollars. The son told his father the coins were found on the bank next to the stream.

Several days later, the son, accompanied by his father, returned to the stream to try to find more of the coins. Though they searched for hours, the exact location of the earlier discovery could not be found.

In 1987 another George Washington dollar was found. A woman driving west on Connecticut's Highway 20 had a flat tire a few yards before reaching the bridge that spanned the East Fork of Salmon Brook. After changing the flat, she walked down to the stream to wash her hands and, while kneeling at the bank, spotted a glittering round object in the stream gravel a few feet away. After retrieving it, she discovered it was a coin. When she had it identified several days later, she learned it was a gold George Washington dollar.

Many who have researched this tale are convinced that the wooden chests containing the George Washington dollars have long since rotted away during the more than two centuries since they were buried in the moist ground. It is likely that decades of flooding, stream undercutting, and bank erosion could have exposed the burial site, causing all or some of the coins to tumble into the rushing waters of the East Fork of Salmon Brook. Since gold is relatively heavy and does not travel far except in the swiftest of streams, there is a distinct possibility that the bulk of the treasure is lying in or close to the brook a relatively short distance upstream from its junction with Highway 20. If found, the treasure is estimated to be worth tens of millions of dollars at today's values.

THE SUNKEN
CONTINENTAL DOLLARS

The *Defense* was a three-masted American frigate that boasted thirty-two cannons and a veteran crew. When all of the sails were raised, this sturdy, well-built ship ran low in the water and coursed along the ocean surface at impressive speeds. Extremely maneuverable, the *Defense* had earned a reputation for avoiding and escaping enemy ships.

During the night of November 11, 1779, the *Defense* bobbed in the choppy waters of an anchorage on the north side of Fishers Island, a long, narrow strip of land just off the southeastern coast of Connecticut. Separating Fishers Island from the Connecticut shore was the two-mile-wide expanse of Fishers Sound. On the seaward side of Fishers Island, an approaching storm was generating treacherous, wind-tossed waves. The captain of the *Defense* paced back and forth along the deck, his eye on the menacing squall line with thick, dark clouds moving in from the southeast. Just behind the looming squall line, the captain knew, a violent gale blew, the kind known to sink ships.

The captain was faced with a vitally important decision, and the oncoming bad weather was not making his choices easy. As the captain peered into the bleak, gloomy blackness and then glanced at the growing whitecaps in the cove, he also scanned the horizon in search of pursuing British warships. The captain was aware the British Navy had information that the *Defense* was nearby, and he also knew that they had knowledge of the rich cargo stored in its hull—500,000 silver coins. The coins were Continental one-dollar units, all packed into several wooden chests. Each of the dollars had been minted only three years earlier, and they were bound for the port at New York and thence on to the treasury of the young nation fighting for its independence.

The captain feared it was just a matter of time before the warships of the British Navy arrived and discovered the *Defense* anchored in the protective cove. If that happened, the *Defense* would be outnumbered, outmanned, and outgunned, and was sure to fall into the hands of the enemy. The captain was unwilling to allow his mission to deliver the funds to be subverted. He had to decide whether to face a large enemy in a pitched, and fruitless, battle, or attempt to flee and deal with the oncoming violent storm. He decided his best chance lay with tackling the storm.

Following a great deal of deliberation, the captain ordered his crewmen to raise the sails and hoist the anchor, all to the strong objections from his crew. To sail into the teeth of the storm was certain death, they pleaded. The captain assured them that the alternative, capture by the British, would result in a certain execution. With the storm, he told them, they had a small chance; with the British, they had none. It was an anxious and concerned crew that set about preparing the *Defense* to sail.

A short time later, with the anchor raised, the sails hoisted, and the strong winds billowing the large rectangular canvases, the *Defense* moved swiftly out of the protective cove and into the waters of Fishers Island Sound. The great weight of the wooden chests filled with the silver coins, along with tons of supplies and other goods, caused the ship to sit low in the water. The dangerous, choppy waves encountered in the sound caused the captain great concern as the ship moved away from land and into the open, tossing sea. He told his first mate that, if God was on their side, they just might be able to outrun the storm before it grew much worse and arrive safely at New York harbor.

Within moments after the *Defense* sailed past the protective western end of Fishers Island, heavier, more threatening seas were encountered. While protected by the cove on the north side of the island, the captain could not have known of the rapidly growing intensity of the approaching storm. Once out of the shadow of the island, the surging, slashing waves tore at the *Defense*, which was riding dangerously low in the water. The powerful waves crashed repeatedly over the bow, tearing equipment and fittings loose from the deck and filling the hold with seawater.

Once in the open sea of the Atlantic, the captain of the *Defense* noted the storm-ravaged skies darkening even more. As he clutched tight to a railing to keep from being swept away by the waves, he watched his nervous crew fight to hold a steady westward course for New York harbor. At one point, the captain feared for the safety of his vessel and crew and decided to retreat back to the cove, but the crewmen were unable to turn the ship in the strong winds and raging sea.

As the captain made his way across the deck shouting encouragement to his charges, the tiller snapped and all control of the vessel was lost. As the *Defense* drifted rudderless and appeared to be taking on more and more water, the captain ordered the sails to be lowered lest the strong winds force the ship over on its side.

It turned out to be too late for the maneuver to save the ship. As the crew worked furiously to lower the sails, the winds intensified, forcing the out-of-control *Defense* farther out to sea. The towering, storm-tossed waves swept across the deck, often displacing men and material and sweeping them into the water.

For almost an hour, the men of the *Defense* fought the storm a few hundred yards from the western tip of Fishers Island. Suddenly, one of the masts snapped in the high wind. Minutes later, the other two broke away. To add to the growing problems, the hull of the vessel began to come apart.

Merciless waves pounded the remains of the *Defense* without cease. Tossed and pitched about in the rolling, violent sea, the ship was slammed into an underwater shoal, the keel mired firmly in the bottom sands. The storm's winds and surging waves struck the vessel broadside, causing it to lurch sideways. At that moment, the lashings securing the heavy coin-filled chests snapped. With the ship floundering at a precarious forty-five degree angle, the weight shifted to the port side, and the sudden redistribution caused the *Defense* to tip even more, taking on seawater at a rapid rate.

Now convinced that the *Defense* was doomed, the captain and crew jumped into the raging waters and tried to swim to Fishers Island, some two hundred yards away. Several made it, but many perished in the attempt.

By the time the survivors, including the captain, reached the shelter of a grove of trees on the western shore of the island, the *Defense* had broken free from its perch on the underwater shoal and began drifting toward the southwest. During occasional lightning strikes, the captain, from his position on the island, could see the *Defense* floating toward the swirling storm, the hull riding low in the water. At the same time, a number of residents of Goshen Point on Connecticut's south shore watched in fascination as the treasure-laden ship disappeared into the low dark clouds of the storm, its prow completely submerged. The *Defense*, it was certain, would not remain afloat much longer. Though out of sight from observers when it finally succumbed to the storm and sank, it has been estimated that the *Defense* finally went down in about fifty feet of water some five miles southwest of Fishers Island.

The pressing issues of the Revolutionary War prevented any attempt at salvaging the Continental dollars. By the time the war wound down, the sinking of the *Defense* and the loss of the Continental dollars was largely forgotten by most and relegated to only a few pages in some area journals and history books.

The existence of the 500,000 silver dollars lying on the shallow continental shelf a few miles from Fishers Island was never far from the minds of a few professional treasure hunters and salvage operators. A number of attempts were made to retrieve the treasure during the 1700s, but the strong underwater currents made recovery difficult to impossible, given the technology of the day. At least one diver lost his life in the process.

During the 1800s, pieces of the *Defense* were occasionally found washed up on the south shore of Fishers Island and the mainland. Artifacts from the ship picked up near Goshen Point often revived the tale of the sinking of the ship and generated renewed interest in retrieving the coins. Several attempts at doing so during the latter part of the nineteenth century led to the recovery of more artifacts such as tools, fittings, and armament, as well as pieces of the ship. No coins were ever found.

In 1956, a man named Solomon Weaver was researching aspects of the history of the area when he encountered a reference to the sinking of the *Defense* and the loss of its rich cargo. Weaver spent months gathering information about the incident, became convinced he knew exactly where the ship went down, and decided to search for it himself. He found the remains of the wrecked ship on his third attempt.

Several dives to the floor of the continental shelf were jeopardized by dangerous, tricky underwater currents. While he reached the site of the sunken *Defense* on several occasions, Weaver never located any coins and, after three months of searching, abandoned his quest.

In 1977, a professional salvor from New York made several attempts to explore the wreck of the *Defense*, but he, like Weaver, found himself at the mercy of the underwater turbulence. Discouraged, he finally gave up his search.

During the past few decades, a number of professional treasure hunters and divers have come to Connecticut and Fishers Island to explore the possibilities of retrieving the vast fortune in silver Continental dollars lying on the sea floor only fifty feet below the surface. Each of them believed they would be able to conquer the dangerous, swirling currents, but all of them failed.

Experts have stated that the precise value of the Continental silver dollars lying in the ocean just off Fishers Island is difficult to calculate, but it would undoubtedly be in the millions. Prominent coin collectors, referring to the historical and antique value of the trove, referred to it as priceless.

The most important obstacle to overcome in the quest to retrieve the incredible fortune is the dangerous sea itself. The seductive attraction of wealth and the quest is fraught with hazard and the threat of death. Until some method is devised enabling searchers to reach the bottom to conduct a search in safety, the Continental dollars will continue to lie undisturbed in the sandy Atlantic sea floor.

THE LOST TREASURE
OF THE H.M.S. *HUSSAR*

During November 1780, the H.M.S. *Hussar*, a frigate flying the flag of the British Navy, was carrying a military payroll estimated to be worth between one and two million dollars in gold and silver coins when it struck a rock outcrop in New York City's East River and sank seventy-five feet to the bottom. Though a number of attempts to reach the ship have been made during the past two centuries, the treasure has never been recovered.

The H.M.S. *Hussar*, constructed in 1763, was a 114-foot British Navy frigate. It carried a crew of two hundred, a large contingent of soldiers, and twenty-eight cannons. In addition to kegs, barrels, and trunks containing supplies, arms, and ammunition, in November 1780 the frigate transported ten American prisoners who had been delivered from prison camps in England and intended to be used to barter for the release of an equal number of captured British soldiers. Additionally, deep in the hold of the H.M.S. *Hussar* were several chests containing gold and silver coins intended as payroll funds for British troops stationed in New York at the time.

For several days, the *Hussar* remained anchored in the New York harbor, a position that made the frigate's captain nervous. Earlier, he had received word that the French were intent on capturing the vessel along with the shipment of gold and silver. In fact, a fleet of French warships was known to be in the vicinity, perhaps as close as Rhode Island, about 150 miles away. To compound the captain's apprehension, intelligence informed him that at least six thousand French soldiers, accompanied by hundreds of sympathetic American troops, were at that moment converging on New York City from the north. An attack could occur at any moment.

Because of the imminent danger to the *Hussar*, its men, and the cargo, the ship's captain, along with General Clinton, the British Commander of New York, decided the ship should be moved immediately to a safer, more defensible location. They decided to proceed to a protective cove in Connecticut, several miles up the coast to the northeast.

The most logical route to Connecticut was to sail parallel to Long Island's south shore. Because of the prevailing southerly winds which sometimes blew vessels onto the beach, however, ships electing to follow this route were forced to sail into positions far out to sea. The captain perceived two serious problems with this plan. First, this route would necessitate a significant investment of time and put them off schedule. Second, the distant offshore location would also expose the *Hussar* to an attack in the open sea from the French warships. It was decided, instead, to sail the frigate up the East River and into Long Island Sound between the island and mainland and thence on to the previously decided-upon location in Connecticut.

Though the decision to navigate the East River was sound from a military and tactical standpoint, it also presented a number of serious problems. One reason why the East River had long been avoided by sailing vessels was the presence of tricky, dangerous currents. In addition, dozens of submerged rocky outcrops had been responsible for the sinking of several other ships in the river.

The captain of the *Hussar* employed a New York citizen to assist in piloting the ship up the East River. Having had long experience with the route, the new pilot advised the captain against sailing it. He warned that the draft of the frigate led to the great possibility that it would likely strike any of a number of submerged rock outcrops found just inches below the surface of the river. The captain, believing he had no other choice, urged the pilot to proceed with caution.

After leaving the New York harbor, the *Hussar* passed the southern tip of Manhattan and on up the East River. As the frigate sailed just to the east of the narrow, two-mile long Welfare Island located in the middle of the river, the swift currents began creating problems, and it required the efforts of several crewmen to keep the ship on course in the middle of the channel.

A short distance beyond Welfare Island, the East River flowed through an area known as Hell's Gate, an aptly named section where the waters of Long Island Sound mixed with those of the stream. These strong, swirling currents had been responsible for slamming dozens of smaller vessels against the rocky shoreline cliffs and small islands in this part of the river. Here, a granite ledge, locally known as Pot Rock, extended far into the stream and barely eighteen inches below the surface. Because of the roiling, silt-laden water, Pot Rock could not be seen from the deck of the *Hussar*.

Just after entering Hell's Gate, the prow of the frigate slammed into Pot Rock with shattering impact, splitting several of the hull timbers. At the moment of collision, the captain raced to the pilot house, pushed the pilot aside, grabbed the wheel, and steered the ship back out into the middle of the channel.

From the pilot house, the captain had a clear view of Stony Point Beach on the South Shore of the Bronx. Returning the wheel to the pilot, he directed him to steer the vessel straight toward the beach and shallow water. After relinquishing the wheel, the captain hurried below deck to assess the damage.

The captain was discouraged at what he found, and it was far worse than he feared. Dirty river water was surging into the hold through several breaks in the hull, and the *Hussar* was already listing dangerously to one side. Fearing that the valuable payroll might never be recovered should the frigate sink in these treacherous waters, the captain prayed for a secure landing at the Stony Point Beach as he returned to the pilot house.

Seventy-five feet beneath the surface of the East River in New York near Hell's Gate lies a treasure trove of silver and gold. Library of Congress

It was not to happen. Minutes later, the *Hussar*, its hull almost completely filled with water, ceased its forward movement and rocked uncontrollably in the middle of the river. Aware that sinking was imminent, crewmen lowered lifeboats into the stream and quickly crowded into them. As the last lifeboat was rowed away from the crippled *Hussar*, the frigate went straight down, plummeting to the bottom like a rock. When the crewmen and soldiers finally reached the closest shore, they stared back toward the river and saw only the tops of the *Hussar*'s masts protruding above the water line.

A number of the more dedicated crewmen volunteered to make an attempt to retrieve the payroll, but they were discouraged by the captain who feared the waters were far too treacherous. For the next few years, the British were occupied with the war and undertook no organized attempt to recover the treasure lying at the bottom of the East River at Hell's Gate.

The first serious attempt to recover the gold and silver coins came in 1819. Details are sketchy, but what is known for certain is that several cannons were recovered along with dozens of metal fittings and a variety of ship hardware. About two dozen coins were raised, likely spilled out of the rotted wooden chests, but the bulk of the treasure eluded the searchers.

Sometime during the 1820s, a salvage team (unnamed by history) arrived at Hell's Gate to try to locate and retrieve the payroll. After estimating the location of the sunken *Hussar*, they rowed out into the river at a point above the wreck, unreeled a long cable with grappling hooks into the depths of the muddy water, and returned the other end of the cable to the shore. Here, the cable was attached to a winch and reeled in, dragging to shore several artifacts. However, not a single coin was found.

In 1832, another salvage company, this one from Great Britain, arrived in New York City with the announcement that it would make an attempt to recover the lost payroll of the H.M.S. *Hussar* from the bottom of the East River. During a newspaper interview, the leader of the salvage team stated he intended to employ a new invention called a diving bell. While the bell tested positively in calm waters, it was no match for the violent and unpredictable currents found in Hell's Gate. After several unsuccessful attempts, the salvors packed up and returned to England.

As the years passed, more and more ships were sent to the bottom of the East River at Hell's Gate as a result of Pot Rock. In time, the river bottom was so littered with the wreckage of other vessels that it became impossible to determine which one was the H.M.S. *Hussar.*

Yet another salvage team from England, the Worcester Hussar Company, arrived in New York in 1856. They established headquarters on the eastern shore of the East River opposite of where they determined the wreck to lie at the bottom of the stream. Among the documentation in the possession of the W.H.C. was information from British archives showing that the payroll transported by the *Hussar* totaled 1.8 million dollars in gold and silver coins when it sank. Other documents that surfaced a decade later claimed two million, and yet another found in 1907 stated the *Hussar* was carrying one million in coin.

The Worcester Hussar Company, like the other searchers, encountered the same problems with the swift and vicious river currents. After less than a week of trying to reach the wreck, the W.H.C. gave up.

New York City newspaper headlines of 1937 announced the arrival of inventor Simon Lake. Lake had designed and built a miniature submarine with which he intended to descend to the river's depths and locate the *Hussar.* His search was a failure.

That the wreckage of the H.M.S. *Hussar* and its shipment of gold and silver coins lie at the bottom of the East River at Hell's Gate is not open to question—the cargo was documented and the tragic sinking was witnessed by hundreds. Without doubt, a fortune amounting to some twenty to twenty-five million dollars in today's values lies at the bottom of the river not far from the shore of Astoria Park. Because of the treacherous currents throughout the seventy feet of depth, the treasure will yield only to the most sophisticated of recovery operations.

III

CIVIL WAR

MOREHEAD CITY'S
CONFEDERATE TREASURE

Fort Macon, located on a low barrier island off North Carolina's shore called Bogue Banks, was originally constructed by the Federals. During the War Between the States, both Union and Confederate leaders regarded the tiny outpost as having great strategic importance, even though it was generally manned by no more than twenty soldiers at a time. When first built, the fort contained a number of cannons, all of which were pointed toward the Atlantic waters, always ready to defend against an attack from a Confederate armada or to inflict damage to any Rebel vessel that passed within range.

In 1861, Confederate Captain Joseph Pender, leading a force of fifty troops, captured the fort from the Yankees. For more than a year, Pender's rebel soldiers remained in command of Fort Macon, manning the cannons and occasionally firing upon Yankee ships that strayed too close.

Early in 1862, the Union Army decided to oust the Confederates from Fort Macon. During April of that year, Yankee General Ambrose Burnside received orders to recapture Fort Macon as soon as possible. Burnside assembled two hundred troops along with a number of officers on the North Carolina shore at a site near which present-day Morehead City is located. Fort Macon, built on the eastern end of Bogue Banks, was separated from the mainland by Bogue Sound, approximately one mile of open water.

Though eager to recapture the fort, Burnside was worried about his assignment. His concern was related to the youth and inexperience of the company of soldiers he was to command. None of the men assigned to him, some of whom were still in their teens, had ever seen battle and all were visibly nervous about the approaching fight. Burnside feared their inexperience could jeopardize the outcome of the operation.

Burnside, a shrewd strategist and a strong disciplinarian, was determined that the mission should succeed. To this end, he sent his best scouts over to the island to examine the position of the fort, assess the geography of this part of the island, and report back to him. In the meantime, the general subjected the young soldiers under his command to some intensive training in preparation for the coming assault.

A few days later, the scouts returned with their report. They noted that all of the heavy cannons were pointed seaward in anticipation of an attack from that direction. After spending an evening with the scouts, Burnside decided a surprise attack on Fort Macon from the mainland side provided the best chance for success. The next morning, he ordered several of the soldiers to begin cutting trees and constructing rafts stout enough to transport men and cannons across the sound to the island.

Just before dawn on the day of the planned attack, Burnside assembled his company of soldiers at the point of land where Morehead City is now located. He left the troopers in the charge of one Sergeant Gore while he and several of his lieutenants and captains discussed last-minute battle plans in the command tent.

Gore was a thirty-five-year-old veteran of a half-dozen skirmishes and had been wounded twice. With Burnside and the other officers several dozen yards away and out of hearing range, the sergeant addressed the young soldiers. Walking among the rows and columns of troops, Gore instructed them to remove any and all belongings—rings, watches, jewelry, and money—and place the items in a sack. He told the troopers that the general did not want any valuables to fall into the hands of the Confederate enemy, and that the items would be returned following the recapture of the fort. The soldiers had recently been paid three month's wages in gold coins and had had no opportunity to spend any of it. The truth was that General Burnside was completely unaware of Gore's plan for the soldier's belongings.

Gore told the soldiers to appoint one man whom they could trust to collect their belongings and bury them in a nearby location. A young private named Joseph Poindexter from Pennsylvania was elected for the task, and a few minutes later he was passing among them with a large canvas sack into which they reluctantly dropped their money and other possessions. This done, Poindexter tied the bag off and, accompanied by Sergeant Gore, disappeared into the nearby woods and buried the valuables among the dense, twisted roots of a large cedar tree.

Minutes later, the soldiers were ordered onto the rafts, and as the sun broke over the eastern horizon, they began rowing toward Bogue Bank and Fort Macon. When they landed on the barrier island beach, teams of men set up the cannons and a furious bombardment of Fort Macon

General Ambrose Burnside, whose troopers stashed a cache of jewelry and coins somewhere near Morehead City, North Carolina. Library of Congress

commenced. When General Burnside determined the Confederate defenders were thoroughly weakened and demoralized from the shelling, he ordered his troops over the walls with instructions to kill or capture every Rebel found within.

During the ensuing fight, much of which was at close quarters, dozens of soldiers were killed, Union and Confederate alike. With a superior force, however, it was only a matter of time before Burnside's contingent was victorious. The few surviving Rebels were forced to surrender and Fort Macon fell into Union hands once again.

As an assessment was being made of the Union dead, Private Poindexter was found with the back of his head shot away. Many of the Yankee soldiers harbored suspicions that Sergeant Gore had murdered the young trooper during the attack and suspected that, at the first opportunity, he would return alone to the secluded spot on the mainland and retrieve the sack of valuables for himself. None of the young soldiers, however, had the courage to make a formal charge against the sergeant.

As the troopers debated among themselves how best to deal with the problem of getting their money and valuables returned, General Burnside suddenly received orders to bring his troops back to the mainland in order to support another Union company currently engaged in a fierce battle with Confederate forces only a few miles away. After quickly assembling his men, Burnside had them row back across Bogue Sound and march toward their new assignment. Sergeant Gore, however, was provided a command of ten soldiers and placed in charge of Fort Macon until such time as he could be relieved. Gore learned several days later that nearly all of the soldiers who accompanied General Burnside had been killed in the battle.

Sergeant Gore remained assigned to Fort Macon until the South finally surrendered in 1865. During the last few months of the war, he became quite ill and often endured long and painful fits of violent coughing. With the war over and his release from the army only weeks away, Gore decided the time to retrieve the buried treasure he had hidden four years earlier had arrived. Gore planned to live the remainder of his life in luxury with his ill-gotten gains, and he looked forward to returning to his home a wealthy man.

Markedly weakened by his worsening sickness, Gore hired a local fisherman to row him across the sound to the North Carolina shore. While Gore was stationed at Fort Macon, he and the fisherman spent time gambling and drinking and had become good friends. During the trip across Bogue Sound to the mainland, Gore, still troubled by fits of coughing, told the fisherman about the hidden treasure and offered to share some of it with him.

As they traversed the open water, Gore described the location of the secret cache to his friend, stating the treasure was buried next to a large cedar tree with several thick, exposed roots not far from the shore. The sack of money, watches, and jewelry, he claimed, was buried about eighteen inches below the surface.

When the rowboat finally reached the beach minutes later, Gore was attempting to climb out when he was stricken with another fit of severe coughing. After several minutes, and experiencing a shortness of breath, the sergeant collapsed back into the boat, barely conscious. Concerned that his friend Gore might die before leading him to the treasure, the fisherman picked him up and carried him to the nearby home of a physician. After examining the sick man, the doctor diagnosed his ailment as typhoid fever and recommended he remain for a few days for treatment. Gore never regained consciousness, and died the following morning.

The fisherman, realizing the buried treasure was now his for the taking, went to the area Gore described. To his dismay, he found not one but hundreds of large cedar trees and nothing to distinguish one from the other. For days he dug around the trunks and among the roots of several of them, finding nothing. He eventually gave up and returned to his fishing.

As far as is known, the sack containing the money and valuables of the Union soldiers has never been recovered. The founding and subsequent growth of Morehead City has likely accounted for significant modification of this part of the North Carolina coast such that it bears little or no resemblance to what it looked like during the Civil War.

There remains a great possibility that not far from the shoreline just across Bogue Sound from Fort Macon, an area that is now a North Carolina State Park, there still lies buried what today could be considered a significant fortune in Confederate gold, jewelry, watches, and other items from the Civil War.

THE LOST TREASURE OF THE CONFEDERATE ARMY'S GRAY GHOST

The well-known and colorful Confederate General John Singleton Mosby was called the "Gray Ghost" by the Union soldiers who pursued but could never capture him. Mosby's raids and campaigns of harassment and predation against federal forces made him legendary among the enemy, and tales of his exploits were common for decades after the war.

John Mosby graduated from the University of Virginia in 1852 and became a busy and successful lawyer in Bristol, Virginia. When the War Between the States broke out in 1861, he enlisted in the Southern army as a private, eager to do battle with what he considered the oppressive rule of the Federals. For a time, he served as a scout for General J. E. B. Stuart during what has been called the Peninsula Campaign, and as a result of being recognized for extreme valor at the Battle of Bull Run, he was promoted to colonel. In 1863, Mosby organized and led an elite guerilla unit called Mosby's Partisan Raiders, and with this well-trained team of fearless fighting men, he led endless raids against the Yankees throughout Maryland and Virginia, cutting communications lines, destroying supply trains, and capturing outposts and prisoners.

In 1863, Mosby and his raiders attacked the Fairfax County courthouse in Fairfax, Virginia. Here, they surprised and captured Union General Edwin H. Stoughton. Even though he had been promoted to high rank, Stoughton was never regarded as much of a leader and seldom received the respect of his fellow officers. He has been described as overweight and overbearing and far too obsessed with fine foods, wine, and women to pay much attention to what was going on in the war. A few of the kinder critics wrote that Stoughton lacked enthusiasm for combat; others just called him a coward.

When Mosby and his band of fighters entered the Fairfax County courthouse, they discovered Stoughton had taken it over to use as his private residence for the duration of the war. The fat general surrounded himself with casks of wine and great stores of food, some of which were imported, and in spite of the bloody conflict ensuing around him, he apparently decided to lead a life of luxury and hedonism while sending his men out to fight.

When Mosby encountered Stoughton, the Union general was encircled by two captains and thirty-eight enlisted men. Despite the heavy guard, the general was taken with ease and the Confederates secured the courthouse. In addition to Stoughton and his men, Mosby's Raiders also captured fifty-eight horses, a number of carriages and wagons, dozens of wooden crates containing expensive victuals, and several casks of wines and bourbon. In Stoughton's quarters, Mosby was surprised to find a fortune in gold and silver plate, coins, jewelry, and expensive tableware that the general and his soldiers had stolen from Southern homes and businesses during the previous months. All together, Mosby estimated the value of these goods at around $350,000 at the time. He ordered his men to gather up the valuables and place them in a number of canvas sacks.

A few days later, Mosby's scouts informed him that a large contingent of Union soldiers was searching for him and was only a few miles away. In haste, he ordered his men to load the canvas sacks filled with booty, along with the crates and casks of food and wine, into the carriages. Taking Stoughton and his men as hostage prisoners, the raiders departed Fairfax and fled toward the town of Culpeper, over fifty miles to the southwest. There, he knew, General Stuart awaited his arrival.

Mosby's Raiders, along with their prisoners and cargo in the wagons and carriages, moved through the rolling hills of Virginia's Appalachian Piedmont. When they crossed into neighboring Farquier County, one of the scouts reported to Mosby that a company of Union cavalry was bearing down on them from the northeast. Because the heavy, cumbersome wagons were slowing down the Confederates, Mosby ordered, no doubt to Stoughton's dismay, that the casks of wine and liquor and crates of food be abandoned. Because of their collective great weight, he also decided to bury the sacks of treasure.

As Mosby recalled in later years, the raiders paused briefly about midway between the small Farquier County towns of Haymarket and New Baltimore to unload the excess cargo. While some of his soldiers hurriedly threw the casks and crates to the ground, Mosby, accompanied by his trusted aide, Sergeant James F. Ames, toted the treasure-filled sacks several yards off the main trail, quickly excavated a shallow pit, and deposited the booty within. As Sergeant Ames filled in the hole, Mosby, using his saber, cut slashes into several nearby tree trunks so that this spot could easily be identified on his return. Mosby anticipated passing through this area again in a few weeks, at which time he planned to dig up the treasure and place it in a safer location. As it turned out, his war-related responsibilities kept him occupied, taking him farther and farther away from Farquier County.

Mosby remained busy throughout the rest of the war, and his guerilla force went on to score more victories and harass the enemy. Union forces never succeeding in capturing him. When at last the Civil

Mosby's Raiders are shown looting a Union wagon train in this lithograph from 1863. Library of Congress

War was over, Mosby settled into Warrenton in western Virginia and returned to the practice of law. In 1872, he supported President Grant for reelection. From 1878 to 1885, he served as U.S. consul to Hong Kong. Between 1904 and 1910, Mosby was an assistant attorney for the United States Department of Justice. During this time, he wrote two books about the Civil War. According to his diaries and journals, he never returned to Farquier County to retrieve the treasure he buried there in 1863.

Over the years, other members of Mosby's band told of the great treasure taken from General Stoughton and of burying it somewhere along the road between Haymarket and New Baltimore, Virginia, during the flight from the pursuing Yankees. Though many of the raiders were aware of the treasure, only Mosby and Sergeant Ames knew the exact location where it was buried. Ames, however, was never able to reveal the location because during the war he was captured by the forces of General George Armstrong Custer and hanged at Fort Royal.

Several times during his life, Mosby was asked why he never returned to Farquier County to retrieve the treasure. Invariably, the retired war hero would change the subject. When he was eighty-three years old in 1916, the Gray Ghost was asked again why he never went back to dig up the great treasure. He replied that he "always meant to return to the area and look for the cache we buried after capturing Stoughton. Some of the most precious heirlooms of old Virginia are buried there. I guess that one of these days someone will find it." John Singleton Mosby, the famous Gray Ghost, died in Washington D.C. on May 30, 1916.

Today, it is estimated that the canvas sacks containing the gold, silver, coins, jewelry, and other items would be worth several million dollars. Over the years, treasure hunters have tried to locate the cache along the old road between Haymarket and New Baltimore, but to date it has never been found.

A FORTUNE IN
CONFEDERATE SILVER

The year was 1864, and the Confederate Army was experiencing increasing difficulty maintaining sufficient funds in its treasury in order to purchase arms, ammunition, and supplies, as well as meeting payments for its soldiers in the field. Though documentation is sketchy, enough evidence exists to support the notion that a train, bearing tons of silver ingots intended for the Rebel cause, was traveling through western New York state when it was stopped and robbed. The silver, estimated to be several million dollars' worth, never arrived in the South, and its whereabouts remained a mystery until twenty years later, when it was found and then lost again.

At least eighteen men were sitting horseback and hiding among a grove of trees one night as the treasure-laden train approached a remote location in western New York. The light of a full moon glinted off the railroad tracks, and each of the apprehensive horsemen eyed a large boulder that had been moved onto the rails. The boulder was positioned such that the engineer could see it in time to stop the train. If he did not, it would surely derail.

At the last moment the engineer spotted the huge rock and applied the brakes, but it was too late. Though the speed of the train was dramatically reduced, it was still going too fast to prevent the impending disaster. The engine slammed into the boulder with such force that it, along with the two following cars, was knocked from the track. At that moment, the eighteen horsemen pulled bandannas and scarves over their faces, broke from cover, and spurred their mounts toward the disabled train. In their hands they carried rifles and pistols.

Dazed and injured railroad employees were rounded up and placed under guard. Four of the riders went to one of the boxcars, broke open the wooden door, and climbed inside. There, they looked upon the target of their robbery. Inside the boxcar were hundreds, perhaps thousands,

This cartoon from 1862 shows a beleaguered Jefferson Davis coping with the costs of war. It didn't help matters when several millions of dollars of silver intended for the Rebel cause disappeared on its way to Richmond from western New York. Library of Congress

of silver ingots. Once stacked neatly against one wall of the car, they were now strewn about the floor as a result of the violent collision. A moment later, the leader of the gang of men flashed a signal toward the nearby woods, and seconds later a caravan of a dozen stout wagons, each pulled by a team of four horses, filed out of their hiding place toward the boxcar.

It took the remainder of the night to transfer all of the silver ingots from the boxcar into the wagons. When the job was completed, the wagon drivers drove the vehicles across the railroad tracks and onto a little used dirt road that led into Pennsylvania several miles away. By the time the sun rose, the wagons bearing the silver bars were already twenty miles away from the scene of the crime. It was two days before investigators arrived at the site of the wreck, but by then the trail was cold.

The amount of silver taken from the boxcar that night has been estimated to be at least twenty tons, with some researchers insisting it was closer to 115 tons!

Throughout the ensuing century-and-a-half, the entire train robbery incident has been shrouded in mystery. The source of the silver is unknown, although many are convinced it was gathered and contributed by Northern businessmen sympathetic to the Confederate cause, loaded onto the train, and intended to be clandestinely shipped to some unidentified location in the South. Others insist that the silver was stolen from a Federal depository, but no report of such a theft has ever been found. The large group of men who robbed the train has never been identified, but it is evident that they were in possession of accurate intelligence and that they operated in a disciplined, almost military, manner. The location to which the fortune in silver ingots was transported and for what purpose also remains a mystery, but twenty years after the robbery, evidence has surfaced that suggests it was hidden in a remote cave in Fayette County in southwestern Pennsylvania.

Fayette County lies upon highly jointed and thinly bedded limestone, which is conducive to the formation of caves. Indeed, it has been estimated that hundreds of natural caves exist in the region, and Laurel Caverns, a popular tourist and recreation destination, lies only five miles southeast from downtown Uniontown in Forbes State Forest.

During the mid-1800s, an elderly, white-haired, reclusive trapper named Dobbs lived in a crude cabin of his own making near today's Laurel Caverns. Dobbs generally avoided contact with others and was rarely seen by his few neighbors. He survived principally by foraging for nuts and berries in the woods, snaring rabbits, and trading the few pelts he acquired with his rusty traps for food in Uniontown. About once every month, Dobbs would walk into town and trade for a small sackful of tinned goods. Now and then, he agreed to work odd jobs in town or on nearby farms, and the money he was paid was used to purchase liquor.

One day in 1866, Dobbs arrived in town, went to the grocery store, and filled up an old canvas bag with meats, cheeses, and tins of tomatoes and fish. Surprised, the grocer, who had known Dobbs for years, asked him how he planned to pay for it all. In return, Dobbs handed the proprietor a silver ingot. Astonished at the large, heavy bar, the grocer inquired of the trapper how he'd happened onto such riches. Dobbs casually replied that he had found a cave filled with hundreds of the ingots.

Once every month thereafter, Dobbs arrived in Uniontown to purchase food and other supplies, always paying with a silver ingot. Each of the bars was stamped with the inscription, "Government Genuine, New York City."

Others in town noticed Dobbs's sudden wealth, and at times he was followed after making his purchases. When he suspected someone was on his trail, Dobbs would leave the road and make his way through the thick woods, often doubling back on his tracks to confuse any who might be intent on finding where his ingots were stored. He never approached the cave where the treasure was hidden when he thought someone might be observing him.

In 1869, a group of four hunters rode into Uniontown and made purchases at the mercantile, the grocery store, and the taverns with several bars bearing the same inscriptions as those of Dobbs. When asked, the hunters claimed they found the bars, along with thousands of others, in a cave a few miles southeast of town. They said they intended to return for the rest and live the remainder of their lives as wealthy men.

The following morning, the hunters rode out of Uniontown and were never seen again. It was never known if they returned to the cave and retrieved any more of the silver bars. In 1871, four skeletons were found in the woods not far from Laurel Caverns, and many are convinced that Dobbs discovered the hunters taking silver from the cave and killed them.

A few weeks after the skeletons were found, Dobbs came to Uniontown and announced to all that no one would ever be able to find his fortune because he had moved it to a different location. It was learned later that Dobbs also moved out of his shack and his new residence was unknown.

One day in 1872 Dobbs came to town to make his usual purchases. That evening, he went to a local tavern where he had too much to drink and told an acquaintance that he had transferred all of the silver bars from the cave where he found them to a new location—an abandoned coal mine. So remote was this mine, Dobbs told his friend, that no one would ever be able to find it.

Dobbs continued to come to Uniontown to buy supplies once every month for the next two years. Then, one month he didn't show up. Nor did he the next month. Nor the next. In fact, Dobbs was never seen in Uniontown again, and residents assumed that the old man had met with a fatal accident or finally succumbed to old age. For months afterward, several Uniontown citizens would undertake a search to try to find the abandoned coal mine where Dobbs claimed he hid his treasure, but none were successful.

During the summer of 1873, a man many believe to be Dobbs showed up in Latrobe, a small town some thirty-five miles northeast of Uniontown. The old man, with long, white hair and a generally unkempt appearance, lived under porches and in alleys, and solicited handouts from Latrobe residents. The residents of Latrobe regarded him as a vagrant but generally treated him kindly.

When the old man would finally acquire enough money to purchase a few drinks, he could be seen in the local tavern where, inebriated, he would tell a strange story of how he came to lose a fortune in silver ingots.

According to a story attributed to the vagrant, he had been living above an abandoned coal mine, deep within which he had hidden hundreds of bars of silver. The mine collapsed, burying the bars under uncountable tons of rock. Though the old man tried for weeks to dig through the rubble and reach his cache, he eventually realized it was hopeless.

For another year the old man lived in Latrobe on handouts and odd jobs. One morning, he was found dead in an alley and given a pauper's burial. It was never learned for certain if the old tramp was the recluse Dobbs who once lived near Uniontown and who was wealthy beyond imagination. The man in Latrobe died penniless.

Considering the evidence, there is no basis on which to reject Dobbs's claim that he found an extremely large cache of silver bars. During the 1970s, a California-based treasure hunting company arrived in southwestern Pennsylvania to conduct research on the tale. Firmly convinced that an impressive fortune in silver bars lay in a collapsed coal mine somewhere in the region, they undertook a deliberate and organized search. Several mines were found, many of them dating back to the mid-nineteenth century. Several bores were sunk into these abandoned mines in hope of locating some evidence of the silver, but none was found.

There is no reason to believe that any of Dobbs's silver ingots have ever been found. It is likewise easy to conclude they remain deep within the collapsed coal mine of which the old man spoke. It is logical to assume that the old coal mine was located not too far from the original hiding place near Laurel Caverns, for the task of transferring what amounted to several tons of silver ingots by one man is immense.

The minimum estimate of silver buried in the collapsed coal mine is twenty tons, give or take the thirty or so bars Dobbs used to pay for purchases in Uniontown. If twenty tons of silver are buried there (and there may be more, much more), the value of this lost cache has been estimated at no less than $3,000,000 and perhaps as much as $18,000,000 to $20,000,000, with an antique value ranging much higher.

Dobbs's collapsed coal mine would have been originally dug by hand, since the heavy equipment used for strip mining did not exist at that time. If the old mine could ever be identified with certainty, it may be possible to bring large earth-moving equipment to the site to uncover it. Such would require a significant investment in time and money, but the rewards would be impressive.

CONFEDERATE TREASURE
IN VERMONT

America's Civil War, 1861–1865, was fought over the question of states' rights and significant differences in ideologies as they related to slavery and economics. Eventually, eleven states seceded from the Union and organized into the Confederate States of America, an attempt at creating a separate nation.

The sites of pitched battles between the two forces, important victories and crushing defeats, have been made into national and state parks. Even the locations of lesser skirmishes between the northern and southern forces have been identified and preserved and in many cases made available for tourism, historical research, and recreation.

Few people associate Civil War–related skirmishes with the state of Vermont and the country of Canada, but in 1864, a small company of Confederate soldiers raided a small New England town, stole a fortune in gold from its banks, and fled north into Canada. Most of the gold, all in coin, was buried somewhere along the escape route and the search for it continues today.

Just past midnight on October 18, 1864, a contingent of twenty-five Confederate soldiers broke camp along the banks of Lake Champlain's Missiquoi Bay, saddled their horses, mounted up, and rode single-file southward down a narrow road leading from the Canadian Province of Quebec into Vermont. The morning was cold, the dew heavy on the grass and brush, the riders silent. The only sound that could be heard was the jingling of metal harness fittings and the occasional blow of a horse.

The abbreviated company was led by Captain Bennet H. Young. The destination was St. Albans, a small, quiet village located less than twenty miles from the international border in northwestern Vermont.

Though the Confederacy was composed primarily of Southern states, the government of the Southern resistance maintained a presence in eastern Canada. From this vantage point, safe from the intrusion of the Northern Army, Southerners courted the Canadians as well as friendly Europeans, soliciting monies for arms and ammunition in order to carry on the struggle. By 1864, however, things were looking grim for the South, and desperation raids by small Rebel armies were common, but never this far north of the Mason-Dixon Line.

Young's command was one of several stationed in Canada. On October 15, the captain received coded intelligence describing how large deposits of gold coins totaling $200,000 had been made in each of the three banks in St. Albans. With the South badly in need of money to plug deep holes in the Confederate treasury, Young and his troops were ordered to loot the Yankee banks and move the gold to Canada. From there, it would be shipped to Richmond, Virginia.

Just as the morning sun illuminated the tree line east of St. Albans, the Young-led troopers galloped into town firing weapons and screaming rebel yells. With little trouble, they forced their way into the banks and crammed the $200,000 in gold coins into saddlebags. As they strapped the heavy leather pouches onto spare horses appropriated from a nearby corral, the citizens of St. Albans, awakened by the commotion, were loading their weapons and preparing to defend the village against the mysterious raiders. Before the St. Albanites could determine what was happening, the Rebels, still shooting off their weapons, set fire to the banks, mounted up, and escaped northward. The entire raid took less than thirty minutes.

By the time the Confederates were picking up speed on their way out of town, armed St. Albans citizens were pouring into the streets searching for something to shoot at. Several shots were fired at the retreating horsemen but none found their mark. Return fire from the soldiers, however, hit two of the residents; one was killed, the other seriously wounded.

On the trail north of town, Young, fearful of pursuit, urged his soldiers to greater speed. He was desperate to get his command back across the border before an effective posse could be organized.

Within minutes after the robbery, however, about thirty angry, vengeance-minded St. Albanites were already whipping their horses along the same trail taken by the bank robbers.

Up ahead, the raiders were experiencing serious problems with the pack animals they were using. The horses, unaccustomed to carrying the heavy weight, were tiring and slowing down. Further, the Confederates were unskilled in close-herding the animals, and the frenzied activity made the horses skittish. Every now and then one of the horses would break away, only to be chased down and returned to the column. On at least two occasions, the command was forced to stop when two of the hastily secured, gold-filled saddlebags broke loose and fell to the ground.

The troops were only two miles from the border. Concerned about the recurring problems slowing down the escape and acutely aware that pursuers were only minutes away, Young ordered several of the saddle-bags removed from the horses and buried in a pine grove he spotted just off the trail. With haste, five troopers excavated a shallow hole, placed the saddlebags within, and covered them over. Nearby was a large flat rock. Young enlisted four of the men to carry the huge rock to the cache and place it over the top. The soldiers struggled but finally succeeded in drop-ping the rock on top of the site. At that moment, Young heard the sound of pursuing horses on the trail behind them. Quickly, the Rebels mounted up and quirted their tired mounts onward.

A short time later, the Southerners crossed the international border with the posse in sight behind them. Believing they were safe, the rebel troops slowed their horses to a walk, turned, and jeered at the Vermon-ters they believed they had just outwitted.

Much to Young's surprise, the St. Albanites did not stop at the bor-der, but galloped their horses even faster in an attempt to reach the raiders. With the angry Vermonters nearly on top of them, Young's men, now in fear for their lives, tried to coax their own mounts to greater speeds.

Within seconds, three of the Southerners fell to Yankee bullets. Young, believing his only chance was to fight, ordered his men to turn and draw weapons. During the ensuing skirmish, ten more Rebels were killed, eleven captured, and only three managed to escape.

When the saddlebags were searched, the Vermonters found only $80,000 of the stolen gold coins, and they deduced that the Confeder-ates must have buried the rest somewhere along the trail. On the return trip, the posse members scanned both sides of the trail for some sign of a recent excavation or a likely place to cache several saddlebags worth of gold but found nothing. None of the captured Rebel soldiers were with the detail assigned to bury the gold, so they could provide no insight into the location. The search for the missing coins continued for weeks but was finally abandoned when it appeared hopeless.

The details of the Confederate raid on St. Albans was widely re-ported. As time passed, it was relegated to a minor role in the history of the Green Mountain State and, save by those who lost money or suffered the deaths of relatives, was soon forgotten.

Four years later, a former Confederate soldier lay dying from tuberculosis in a Greenville, Mississippi, hospital. All efforts to save his life had failed, and it was only a matter of days, perhaps hours, until he succumbed. During a visit to the man's bedside, a doctor asked if there were any relatives that needed to be notified. The soldier, too weak to speak, shook his head, then reached under his sheets and withdrew a diary, which he handed to the physician. The doctor placed the small, worn journal in a pocket, then left to tend to other patients.

That evening, the ex-soldier died. He was buried the following day in a pauper's grave with no one in attendance save for a minister, one city official, and two grave diggers.

A week passed before the doctor had an opportunity to examine the dead soldier's diary. What he read stunned him. It provided a detailed account of the St. Albans raid, the preparations leading up to it, and the aftermath. It described in detail the burying of the $120,000 worth of gold coins just a few yards off the St. Albans–Montreal road, and the placing of a very heavy flat rock on top of it.

According to the dead man, he was one of the three Rebels who escaped from the St. Albans posse in October 1864. Not wishing to return to the Confederate headquarters in Montreal, he decided to desert and return to his home in Mississippi. Shortly after the fight, he rode into the woods and turned toward the southwest. For days on end, he rode, avoiding settlements and travelers. After two weeks, his horses gave out and had to be abandoned. On foot, he eventually made his way to the Ohio River somewhere in Indiana. From there, he hitched a series of boat rides to the Mississippi River where he built a crude raft and floated southward with the current until finally reaching his Greenville, Mississippi, home.

The doctor, with visions of growing rich from recovering the hidden gold coins, began to make plans to travel to Vermont to search for the location. His position with the hospital, however, kept him busy, and he was never able to manage the time. He held on to the diary for years, then, realizing he would never be able to make the journey, passed it along to a friend. The diary went through several more ownerships over the next several years before landing in the possession of one Hubert Crane in 1908. Crane, a resident of Birmingham, Alabama, was keenly interested in Civil War history and, having read the diary of the dead Confederate soldier, became obsessed with finding the buried treasure of coins. As soon as he could make the appropriate arrangements, he traveled to St. Albans, Vermont.

On arriving, Crane checked into an established, historic hotel in town and began asking questions of some of the old-timers about the 1864 raid on the banks. Only a handful of people were left in town who were alive in 1864. Their memories were dim and their versions of the event conflicted. None were involved in the pursuit of the Rebels into Quebec.

Crane read reports of the event in old newspapers and soon realized the conclusions were all the same. Approximately $120,000 worth of gold coins was buried a few yards off the old St. Albans–Montreal road about two miles south of the Canadian border. There was nothing to do but go search for the treasure himself. There was one major aspect of the search he regarded as vital—he had to find the large flat rock that was placed over the cache, one that required four troopers to move it into place. This shouldn't be too difficult, he told himself.

For days, Crane searched the sides of the road in a broad region he identified as having potential. He found not one, but many pine groves. The area he selected to search was large, and each day he explored a section of it. Try as he might, however, he was never able to locate the flat rock.

One evening during the second week of his stay in St. Albans, Crane was dining at a local restaurant when he was approached by an old man who politely introduced himself and requested permission to sit and chat. He said he had a story to tell about the buried gold coins.

Crane welcomed the old man, a native of St. Albans, and listened to his tale. He told Crane that sometime during the year 1868, a stranger arrived in town and checked himself into the same hotel where Crane was registered. Like Crane, this newcomer asked many questions of the residents about the stolen gold and other events associated with the 1864 robbery and flight of the Rebel soldiers back into Canada. Otherwise, he remained quiet and withdrawn.

The stranger, who had a very pronounced Southern accent, rented a horse and wagon from the local livery and spent the greater part of each day exploring the area near the road north of town and just south of the Quebec border. Occasionally, travelers along this road reported seeing the man digging in a grove of pines about two miles south of the boundary line.

One afternoon, a suspicious farmer approached the stranger and demanded he explain what he was doing digging in the woods. The stranger offered evasive answers and appeared confused and unsure of where he was and what he was doing. The farmer, believing the newcomer was daft, left him alone thereafter. More time passed, and the stranger left town, carrying only the battered suitcase he arrived with.

According to Crane, the old man who related this story said the stranger revealed that he was one of the three men who escaped from the St. Albans posse and that he had returned to retrieve the buried gold. How the old man knew this was never made clear.

The old man also admitted to Crane that he, himself, had searched many times for the flat rock that allegedly covered the gold cache, but was never successful.

Crane then asked the old-timer if he would guide him out to the location that had been searched so that the two of them could look around. Crane was convinced that the flat rock had long been covered over with dirt and forest debris. He planned to mark off a likely region into grids and search each one separately, using a length of thin metal rod to jab into the soft ground in an attempt to locate the rock. The old man agreed to take him out to the area.

The next morning, Crane leased a horse-drawn carriage, picked up the old man, and drove out to the region in question. On arriving at the approximate site of the treasure cache, both men were surprised and stunned to discover the entire area had been burnt over by an extensive forest fire only a few days earlier. Two hundred acres of woods had been destroyed and not a tree left standing.

The pine grove that many believed was the location of the treasure site no longer existed, and the old man was unable to identify even an approximate location. Dejected, Crane turned and drove back to St. Albans. He returned home to Alabama the following day.

As far as anyone knows, the trove of $120,000 in 1860s-era gold coins buried by the raiding Confederates has never been found, and to this day many are convinced that it still lies only a few inches below the surface somewhere in the second-growth timber north of St. Albans and just a couple of miles south of the Canadian border. Most who have researched the tale believe that it still lies beneath a large, heavy flat rock just a few yards to the left or right of Interstate 89 and not far from the small community of Highgate Springs.

The cache, if located today, is estimated by coin collectors to be worth in the tens of millions of dollars in real and antique value.

POTS OF GOLD

There exist several tales about the final resting place for much of the Confederate treasury, an estimated millions of dollars' worth of gold and silver, mostly in coins. One of the most provocative stories carries with it some compelling documentation. Even more intriguing, a small portion of this treasure has been found in North Carolina, and the rest, believe it or not, may be comparatively easy to locate and recover.

During the autumn of 1864, it was growing increasingly clear that the army of the Confederacy was losing the War Between the States, in part because it was running out of money. Though it has been estimated that the Confederate treasury contained several million dollars during this period, it was not going to be enough to sustain the fight. A number of Southern leaders, aware that the war was winding down, turned their interests toward saving what was left of the treasury instead of winning battles. To that end, much of the wealth that was intended for the purchase of arms, ammunition, supplies, mounts, and payment for the troops was removed from the facility in which it was stored in Richmond, Virginia, and hidden in various locations south of the Mason-Dixon Line so it would not fall into the hands of the Union forces.

One such series of caches in North Carolina is remarkable for its value, estimated to be in the millions, and for the fact that its several locations are known to within a few yards. The tens of thousands of gold coins, packed in common kitchen cooking pots, lie only inches beneath the surface in soft Carolina dirt.

Captain J. W. Duchase, the commander of Company C of the Fourth Mississippi Infantry, was stationed in Richmond during the latter part of 1864. Around 2:00 A.M. one morning, he was awakened from his slumber and told to report immediately to headquarters. After arriving moments later, he encountered officers and aides frantically making

As Richmond, Virginia, came under siege from Union forces in 1864, pots of gold coins were removed from the Confederate capital and hidden throughout the South. While a few have been found, it's possible that several hundred remain undiscovered. Library of Congress

preparations to abandon the area in the wake of news that Union forces were rapidly closing in. Duchase was given orders providing him and his command with the responsibility of moving a significant portion of the South's store of gold coins, transporting them out of the area, and burying them in predetermined locations in North Carolina. Duchase and his entire company were told to report to the Richmond railroad station at 6:30 that evening. Each man was to carry three days' worth of rations, at least forty rounds of ammunition, and full marching gear.

At the appointed time, Duchase and his seventy-eight fighting men were assembled at the platform of the train station. Sitting on the tracks before them was a train consisting of an engine, four boxcars, and three flatcars. The boxcars, Duchase was informed, contained rifles, cannons, ammunition, and other supplies the Confederate leaders thought important to ship far from the encroaching Yankees. The end flatcar carried a three-inch-bore field cannon, some armament, and a detachment of soldiers. The two remaining flatcars were loaded with iron cooking pots, each filled with gold coins from the Confederate treasury, the lids tightly fastened with wire.

As Duchase and his men waited patiently near the train, he was handed a set of orders and told to open them only when he arrived at his assigned destination—Greensboro, North Carolina. On arriving at Greensboro the following day at around 4:00 P.M., Duchase opened his orders and read them. In part, they stated:

> You are to proceed the following night to McLeansville by way of the North Carolina Railroad. After leaving McLeansville, you will bury these pots in groups of three on each side of the railroad tracks and not over one hundred paces from the right-of-way. In case there are houses nearby, proceed further. Also, plot the burial places as nearly as possible.

Duchase and his men followed the instructions to the letter. The train proceeded slowly through the largely uninhabited countryside, stopping often so that soldiers could carry the pots of gold one hundred paces from the track. The pots were buried in groups of three along approximately sixteen miles of railroad track between McLeansville, North Carolina, and a town called Company Shops, later renamed as Burlington.

With the mission completed, Duchase and his troops rode the train in to Company Shops, turned it around at the roundhouse, and returned to McLeansville, then on to Greensboro. From there, they boarded another train to return to Richmond where the Captain was to submit his report on the locations of the buried Confederate gold and contribute to the defense of the city should it be necessary. During the return trip, however, the train was derailed by Union saboteurs and most of the company was captured. Only Duchase and one lieutenant managed to elude the Federals, but during the escape the captain lost the written description of the locations of the buried gold.

Duchase and the lieutenant hid in the woods for several weeks, foraging on wild foods and occasionally stealing or begging food from farms they encountered. With their uniforms in tatters, a gaunt and emaciated Duchase and his companion were on the verge of starvation and sleeping in a hollow log when they were found and captured by Union soldiers. The two men were interrogated, then sent to a prison camp where they remained throughout the duration of the war.

After the South surrendered, Duchase, along with thousands of other imprisoned rebel soldiers, was freed. A short time later, he traveled to Mexico where he invested in copper mining and real estate ventures. Over the years, Duchase grew prosperous, married a Mexican woman, and raised a family. The former Confederate officer thought often of returning to North Carolina to retrieve the millions of dollars' worth of gold coins he buried, but pressing business concerns and family matters demanded his time and he was unable to travel. He was convinced he remembered enough of the area between Greensboro and Company Town to easily relocate most, if not all, of the caches.

While living in Mexico, Duchase began writing about his experiences in the Civil War and in particular his unique assignment relative to hiding the pots of Confederate gold. His writing style was fluid and descriptive, and the details pertaining to where he hid the gold were clear and precise.

More time passed and, as Duchase grew more prosperous in Mexico, his desire to return to the United States lessened. His notes and writings on the war, along with the remembered directions to the buried Confederate gold, were given to a man named P. H. Black, a former resident of Greensboro, North Carolina, who came to Mexico and chanced to meet Duchase during the 1890s. When Black returned to the United States, he carried Duchase's journals.

Around 1900, Duchase passed away in Mexico, having never returned to the United States after leaving thirty-five years earlier. P. H. Black died in North Carolina sometime during the 1930s. When his possessions were divided up among his relatives, the notes from Duchase were not among them and no one knows what became of them. It is also unknown whether or not Black attempted to retrieve any of the gold-filled kitchen pots buried along the railroad tracks between McLeansville and Burlington, North Carolina. If he did, history shows he did not find all of it.

During the 1880s, the town of Burlington grew to become an important industrial settlement in that part of the Appalachian Piedmont region. Out from Burlington and along the tracks of the old North Carolina Railroad, farmers responded to the growing demand of cotton and corn by turning thousands of acres over to prime farmland.

Late one afternoon during the spring of 1910, a black farmhand was plowing in a corn field about three miles west of Burlington. The work was slow and tedious and the day was hot. Both man and horse were tired and looking forward to quitting time. Suddenly, the horse-drawn steel plow struck something hard in the ground, breaking the point. The farmhand dug into the ground and pulled to the surface a heavy rusted iron cooking pot, the lid wired down tightly. When he removed the wire and lid, he was surprised to discover that the pot was filled to the top with twenty-dollar gold pieces. The find was approximately one hundred paces from the railroad tracks.

Unaware of the value of the coins, the farmhand carried several of them into Burlington the next day and traded them for dimes. The gold coins aroused a great deal of curiosity among the local residents, who located the black man and asked him about his discovery. Before the end of the day, the cornfield was swarming with men digging in the ground searching for more pots of gold. Within inches of the pot dug up by the farmhand, the landowner found two more. Though he never told anyone of his discovery until many years later, the landowner was a rich man from that day on.

The three pots of gold recovered from the cornfield near Burlington were the result of luck or accident or both. Others may have been recovered, but the finders likely kept the discoveries to themselves. It is more likely that most of the gold-filled cooking pots, hundreds of them, still lie buried approximately one hundred paces from the old NCR tracks, and that today several million dollars' worth of gold coins lie only a few inches below the surface in the North Carolina dirt.

Author's note: A version of this story was published in a magazine during the mid-1990s. Within a few weeks after the issue came out, a man called me, and identified himself as a professional treasure hunter who had designed and constructed what he referred to as a revolutionary new type of metal detector. He was vitally interested in the story of the buried pots of Confederate gold in North Carolina and was convinced he would be able to find some of them. He asked me if I would share any additional information I had regarding the locations, which I did. Three months later, the man called back and reported he had located and retrieved six of the pots of gold and was hopeful of finding others. A few weeks later he mailed me a sizeable check representing, as he explained, my "consultation fee" for aiding in his discovery. Within the next three years, he found six more pots, each discovery followed by another check. In 2001, I learned the treasure hunter passed away, leaving his family an impressive inheritance. The treasure hunter found, according to his letters, a total of twelve pots of gold in four different locations. Significantly, hundreds more of the gold-filled pots remain to be discovered, all just paces from the old North Carolina Railroad bed.

THE LOST
CONFEDERATE TREASURY

As the end of the Civil War was growing near, there were several attempts made to remove the Confederate treasury from its Richmond, Virginia, storage facility to a safer location. Like the previous tale, this one also carries with it some documentation.

During the final days of the Civil War, Confederate leadership was in disarray, with many ranking officers abandoning their commands and fleeing for safety. The defense of the hopeful young nation was in jeopardy, in large part, because the treasury was rapidly running out of money. Confederate President Jefferson Davis and his cabinet held their final meetings in April 1865 in Abbeville, South Carolina, and Washington, Georgia, as the officers and several politicians escaped from the oncoming Union soldiers.

Though badly depleted as a result of war expenditures, the Confederate treasury remained a significant store of gold and silver coinage. Fearful that the powerful and encroaching Union forces would seize the wealth, the leaders ordered it removed from the temporary treasury located at Richmond, Virginia, and transferred to a more southerly site in order to protect it. Some historians of a cynical nature have hypothesized that the soon-to-be deposed leaders of the Confederacy simply wanted the wealth transferred to a location where they could more easily get their own hands on it should the South find itself defeated by the Yankees, a possibility that was growing stronger with each passing day.

General Robert E. Lee advised Southern President Jefferson Davis that Union General Grant's forces had penetrated Rebel lines at Petersburg and that Richmond was about to be captured. Davis, concerned about the treasury, ordered the city evacuated at once. He assigned Captain William H. Parker the responsibility of removing the treasure and transporting it to a safe location.

Parker, an officer in the Confederate Navy, seemed an unlikely choice for such an important assignment, but he undertook it with his usual air of confidence and seriousness. With the help of some sixty naval midshipmen commandeered from a training vessel anchored on the nearby James River, Parker had the entire remaining wealth of the Southern treasury loaded into a boxcar. Little did he know that it was the first of what would turn out to be many transfers of the precious cargo across four states and hundreds of miles.

At midnight, the train departed Richmond carrying what Parker inventoried as approximately one million dollars in gold and silver coin. During the ensuing years, other estimates for the wealth of the Confederate treasury have ranged as high as thirty million dollars, but this seems unlikely and there exists little evidence to support such claims.

When the train reached Danville in south-central Virginia near the North Carolina border, Parker received orders to proceed southwestward and carry the treasure on to Charlotte where it was to be unloaded at the abandoned United States Mint located there. With his usual efficiency, Parker fulfilled his obligation, but no sooner was the last chest of coins stacked inside the mint when the captain learned from intelligence that Stoneman's cavalry was at that very moment bearing down on this location and that General George Stoneman himself, former chief of cavalry for General Joseph Hooker's Army of the Potomac, was vitally interested in the Confederate funds.

Parker immediately ordered the chests of gold and silver removed from the mint, packed into barrels and sacks of coffee, sugar, and flour, and reloaded onto the train. This done, Parker told the engineer to fire up the boilers and proceed in a southerly direction only to learn that the railroads were out of service just a mile beyond Charlotte. Returning to the boxcar, Parker had his charges unload the barrels and sacks and place them into wagons.

As the treasure was being loaded onto a number of wagons commandeered from a local livery, Parker learned that Varina Davis, the wife of President Jefferson Davis, was currently living in Charlotte with her three children. Parker located her, warned her of the approaching Yankee forces, and insisted she and her children travel south with his military escort.

On April 16, Parker and his men, along with Mrs. Davis and her children and the wagons carrying the Confederate treasury, arrived at Newberry, South Carolina, some seventy-five miles southwest of Charlotte. Here, Parker learned the trains were running again. Buoyed by this news, Parker ordered the coin-filled barrels and sacks carried from the wagons and placed into another boxcar. From Newberry, the party continued on to Abbeville, about fifty miles to the west.

When the detachment reached Abbeville, Mrs. Davis informed Parker she was leaving the train to remain with acquaintances living here. Parker, convinced the Union army was close and in pursuit of the treasure, pleaded with her to continue on with him but she refused. Growing more and more apprehensive about his responsibility to the treasure, Parker decided to abandon the area immediately and travel on to Washington, Georgia, a few miles across the Savannah River to the southwest. Why Parker selected this tiny northeast Georgia town is not clear. Since the trains did not continue in that direction, Parker once again had the gold and silver coins transferred from the boxcar and stacked into more wagons. After bidding Mrs. Davis good-bye, he led his command across the river and into Georgia.

Parker, aware that this part of Georgia had not suffered much at the hands of the invading Yankees, hoped to locate a large Confederate military unit that was capable of taking command of the treasury. The captain had grown frustrated with his responsibility and anxious to transfer it to someone else.

When he arrived in Washington, Parker learned that a company of some two hundred Confederate soldiers were holding Augusta, about fifty miles way to the southeast. He determined he would take the wealth there and turn it over to the officer in charge.

Parker's contingent was running low on food and supplies, and while in Washington, he traded flour and coffee to the residents for eggs and chickens in order to feed his men. After a few hours of rest, the captain once again ordered the gold and silver loaded into a railroad car and instructed the engineer to proceed to Augusta.

At Augusta, Parker discovered that transferring responsibility for the treasure was a difficult proposition. The officers he found there provided the news that the war was over and that the soldiers remained there only to arrange an orderly surrender of the town when the Yankees arrived. Following that, they intended to receive their pay and return to their homes. Having the Confederate treasury in their possession, they informed Parker, would only complicate the process and they wanted nothing whatsoever to do with it.

One of the officers suggested to Parker that he turn the wealth over to the civilian leaders of the Confederate government who were, at that moment, fleeing Union soldiers across the Savannah River into Georgia.

Among those being pursued, the officer told Parker, was President Jefferson Davis himself.

For what he considered compelling reasons, Parker decided that Abbeville, South Carolina, was the best place to find President Davis and inquire about what to do with the treasure. He was convinced Davis knew his wife and children were there and that he would try to find them before escaping into Georgia. The quickest route to Abbeville was back through Washington, so Parker ordered the engineer to return in that direction. Once back at Washington, Parker oversaw the transfer of the treasure from the train once again back into the wagons. Following a brief stop, the journey to Abbeville was underway.

Parker had not been gone from Washington for an hour when, to his surprise, he encountered Mrs. Davis and her three children, along with a small cavalry escort, coming up the road from Abbeville. When the captain inquired about her husband, she told him she had not seen him and had no idea where he could be.

On April 28, Parker and his weary command finally arrived at Abbeville, South Carolina, unloaded the gold and silver coins from the wagons, and had them stored in an empty warehouse just outside of town. He then appointed several men to stand guard around the building.

That evening as he was eating dinner, Parker learned from one of his scouts that a large contingent of Union soldiers was approaching the town from the north and would arrive within two hours. Hastily, Parker assembled his men and ordered them to carry the barrels and sacks of gold and silver from the warehouse and load them into a railroad car. As soon as this was accomplished, he told the engineer to prepare for departure. Before this process could be completed, however, several hundred mounted troopers appeared at the north end of town and riding straight toward the train.

Parker's heart fell and he was prepared to surrender when he discovered the newcomers were not Federals after all but Confederate soldiers. He was further delighted when he learned they were escorting President Jefferson Davis and what was left of his cabinet. Parker raced to greet Davis and informed him of the great misfortunes and difficulties he had encountered while protecting the treasure. To Parker's relief, Davis relieved him of his duties and placed the responsibility for the wealth in the hands of John C. Breckenridge, the secretary of war. Breckenridge, a Kentuckian, was a former vice president of the United States and had served in the Mexican War. He was once nominated for the presidency of the Confederacy.

Breckenridge was not in the least bit enthusiastic about this new charge, and at the first opportunity passed the responsibility of the gold and silver on to General Basil Duke. Duke was likewise unhappy about his new duty but he had no one to pass it on to. Duke, a somewhat pompous officer, assumed his new assignment with his customary military bearing and dignity.

Duke was one of the few remaining Confederate generals, and to his utter disgust he was given a command of almost one thousand poorly armed, poorly equipped, and poorly trained volunteers who were lacking discipline and deserting in droves. When Duke's troops heard that the war had ended, they slipped away by the dozens to return to their farms and families throughout the South.

At around midnight on May 2, Duke ordered his men to transfer the gold and silver from the boxcar to a number of wagons. Earlier that evening, Duke learned that several Union patrols were in the area, and he was determined to move the treasure farther south in order to distance it from the advancing Yankees.

Duke was convinced the Federal officers were certain the treasure was in Abbeville and were determined to seize it. With what remained of his rag-tag force, Duke led the treasure-laden wagon train out of Abbeville in the dark of night, headed once again for the town of Washington. President Davis and his remaining cabinet members rode along, grateful for the escort. Nervous, Duke stationed several of his trusted soldiers at the rear of the column to keep an eye out for pursuit. Others rode along the flanks prepared to fight off a surprise attack by Yankee forces.

Around midmorning of May 3, Duke ordered a brief rest stop. He promised his soldiers that when they reached Washington they would be paid in gold coins from the very treasury they were escorting. Aware that the war was over and eager to be on their way home, many of the soldiers lobbied for payment on the spot. Many of them expressed concern that the Yankee soldiers might overtake them and seize the treasure before they could be paid. Duke, for his part, was worried that if he paid the soldiers now, they would simply ride away, leaving the treasury unguarded and at the mercy of the Union army.

In the end, however, Duke acceded to their demands, and he had one of his junior officers open a barrel of gold coins and count out thirty-two dollars for every soldier in the command. Once this was accomplished, dozens of soldiers rode away, boldly deserting and confident no one would stop them. With the troops remaining, Duke escorted the treasure-filled wagons back across the Savannah River into Georgia and toward Washington.

Along the trail, Duke received word that a large force of Yankees was only a few minutes behind them and intent on attacking his column and taking the treasure. Duke searched for a way to leave the trail and find a place that was easily defensible.

A few minutes later, he led the column onto a narrow trail to a secluded farm belonging to a man named Moss. Duke had his soldiers take over the farm house and at the same time directed that the gold and silver be unloaded from the wagons and stacked in the kitchen. This done, Duke and his men awaited what they presumed to be an imminent attack from the Yankees. The attack never materialized, and the Union force apparently continued along the main trail without noticing it had been abandoned by Duke's command.

It was an uneasy night that Duke and his soldiers spent at the Moss farm. The following morning, scouts reported no Yankees in the vicinity, so Duke ordered the gold and silver reloaded back onto the wagons. It was transported into Washington without incident.

On arriving once again at Washington, Duke transferred the treasure to Confederate Captain Micajah Clark, appointed as treasurer of the Confederate States of America by President Davis only the previous day. Following this act, Davis, accompanied by his wife and children, fled deeper into the South but was captured a week later.

Secretary of the Treasury Clark decided that his first duty was to count the gold and silver coins. According to the record, Clark recorded the exact amount as $288,022.90, considerably less than what Parker reported removing from the Richmond facility. Clark used some of the gold to pay off more of the troops and had the remainder repacked into wooden nail kegs and boxes.

On May 14, two men identifying themselves as officials representing an important Virginia bank arrived in Washington, Georgia, with a federal order requiring the entire amount of the treasury be turned over to them. The bank, it seems, had a claim on the money, and the two men were commissioned to secure it and transport it back to Richmond.

Assured that the order was legitimate, Clark turned over the entire amount to the two bank representatives. They, in turn, had it loaded onto different wagons. Accompanied by a hastily arranged military escort, they departed for Richmond.

None of the young soldiers comprising the escort had experienced any action during the war and all had little military experience beyond carrying out camp chores and running errands. Concerned about the lack of seasoning associated with the contingent, the two bank representatives were visibly apprehensive as they set out for the long journey.

Within hours after departing Washington, one of the scouts reported they were being tailed by a gang of outlaws composed of Confederate deserters and local bandits. The young troopers grew visibly concerned as the wagon train lumbered toward the Savannah River and they cast nervous glances into the surrounding forest in search of an enemy.

The journey was slow and difficult. On the afternoon of May 24 and after covering only twelve miles since leaving Washington, the contingent pulled into the front yard of the home of Reverend Dionysius Chenault. Chenault directed the troopers to lead the wagons into a large horse corral and arrange them into a tight defensive circle. This done, the guard was doubled and posted around the corral while the rest of the soldiers tried to get some sleep.

At midnight, the band of outlaws struck the Chenault farm. After firing only a few defensive shots, the terrified guards quickly surrendered. The remaining soldiers, as well as the bank representatives, were rounded up and held at gunpoint while the outlaws smashed open the kegs and trunks, removed the gold and silver coins, and stuffed them into their saddlebags and pockets. In their greedy haste, the outlaws spilled thousands of dollars in coins onto the ground. When their saddlebags, pouches, and pockets were filled to overflowing, they mounted up and rode away, horses and riders both having difficulty bearing the heavy plunder.

When dawn arrived, members of the Chenault family returned to the horse corral and retrieved what one of the daughters estimated was over $100,000 worth of gold and silver coins that had been dropped onto the ground. Under direction from their father, the family placed all of the coins they found into several kitchen pots and wooden crates, and buried them next to a nearby small stream, a tributary to the Savannah River.

The fleeing outlaws rode northwest from the Chenault farm toward the Savannah River. Several of the braver Confederate soldiers organized a small posse and decided to pursue the thieves, hoping to be able to retrieve some of the treasure. They were quickly joined by a few law enforcement officials who had been informed of the theft.

Slowed by their heavy loads, the outlaws paused to rest their weary horses in a copse of trees when they spotted the pursuers about a mile away. They quickly dug a shallow pit, filled it with the gold and silver coins, and covered it over with dirt and forest debris. Once they eluded the posse, they determined, they would return to this location and retrieve the treasure.

The chase continued, and the outlaws were overtaken on the morning of the next day, became engaged in a fight with the pursuing forces, and were killed. Before dying, one of them told of burying the coins. He described the location as being just off the trail and close to the south bank of the Savannah River. Though members of the posse spent several days searching for the treasure, it was never found.

Time passed, and no one from either the Union or the late Confederate government ever came to the Chenault farm to claim the remnants of the treasure. Some members of the Chenault family wanted to dig up the portion they buried and use it to pay for and improve the farm, but the Reverend cautioned them against such a thing, claiming the time was not right. Researchers are convinced the treasure buried by the Chenaults was never recovered.

Thirty years later, in 1895, retired officer William H. Parker wrote that he suspected Treasurer Micajah Clark submitted a falsified account and kept the balance of the treasury for himself. A few historians are convinced that Confederate President Jefferson Davis, before turning the Confederate treasury over to Captain Parker, removed much of the wealth and kept it himself, burying portions of it along the route of his flight from Richmond to Georgia, mostly between Charlotte and Abbeville. Much, if not all, of it may still lie there today.

During the early decades of the twentieth century, a number of researchers became interested in finding and recovering the portions of the Confederate treasure buried on the Chenault farm and that cached by the fleeing outlaws on the bank of the Savannah River. The search continues, but it is made more difficult today because this region has been inundated by the waters of Clark's Hill Lake. According to a representative from the U.S. Army Corps of Engineers, the portion of the Confederate treasure buried on the Chenault farm is now under thirty feet of water. With advances in underwater diving gear and electronic metal detectors, the possibility remains that these locations could be found. If that should happen, the finder would likely be more than a million dollars wealthier.

IV

OUTLAW TREASURE

THE LOST TREASURE OF
PEDRO NEVAREZ

D espite that fact that few people have ever heard of him, it has been argued by some that Pedro Nevarez may have been the most notorious and successful outlaw in the history of North America. The story of Nevarez (some accounts list his name as Narvaiz) is a fascinating mix of legend, lore, and fact, and save for his ten-year career as a feared, bloodthirsty highwayman, very little is known about him.

A few researchers believe Nevarez was an Indian, possibly Apache, although there is little to support this notion. Some claim he was Mexican, and still others insist he was a half-breed. Nevarez carried the nickname *Chato* for most of his outlaw life. *Chato* is Spanish slang for "snubnose" or "cut-nose," and according to one of the legends that surround him, he lost a portion of his nose during a knife fight.

Nevarez is one of New Mexico's earliest known outlaws, and he was the leader of a gang of brigands and cutthroats that preyed upon wagon trains and travelers making their way up and down the Rio Grande valley that bisected much of the southern part of the state. The band of outlaws, according to history, was composed of Pueblo and Apache Indians along with a few Mexicans. Between 1639 and 1649, no one was safe along the well-traveled roads that paralleled the Rio Grande near present-day Las Cruces. Not only did Nevarez and his men relieve the victims of their money and gold, it is said they occasionally took prisoners with them back to their hideaway and subjected them to slow and sadistic torture.

Favorite targets of Nevarez and his gang were the caravans and pack trains coming out of Mexico carrying supplies to the Spanish settlements up and down the river, traveling as far north as Santa Fe. The caravans routinely transported food, guns, ammunition, mining equipment, and often gold and silver for use in barter. These pack trains were seldom accompanied by a military escort, thus rendering them vulnerable to attack by land pirates. Following each raid on a supply train, Nevarez and his men would escape to their hideaway deep in Soledad Canyon in a nearby mountain range.

One of Chato Nevarez's most successful raids occurred during April 1649. From a point of concealment among some rocks, the leader and his gang watched as a long, northbound pack train wound its way along the river road. The train was led by a contingent of monks. Months earlier, the party departed the monastery at Alcoman, located some forty miles north of Mexico City. Packed onto the mules were quantities of cups, candle holders, chalices, crucifixes, and statuary, all made of gold and manufactured in Mexico City. They were destined to be distributed among the various missions located along the Rio Grande valley.

Around sundown, the monks guided the caravan into a wooded section along the banks of the river and prepared to make camp for the night. After the pack saddles had been removed from the mules and the animals turned out to graze, the monks began gathering firewood. Nevarez chose this moment to attack. Without warning, he and his men swooped down upon the unsuspecting holy men from a nearby low ridge. The monks, members of the Augustinian Order dedicated to non-violence, were unarmed and offered no resistance.

The outlaws rounded up the mules, replaced the treasure-laden packs, and herded them away toward the east. The band halted after two miles, dismounted, and unpacked the animals in order to examine their newly acquired booty. In addition to the wealth in golden church items, Nevarez was delighted to discover dozens of pouches filled with silver coins.

Chato decided to divide some of the spoils on the spot and proceeded to dole out portions of the silver coins to his men. Following this, the remainder was repacked and transported to the hideout in Soledad Canyon and placed in a cave.

On foot, the Augustinian monks made their way back to El Paso del Norte, the city on the Rio Grande. They reported the robbery to their superiors at the mission there, and a full account of the event was forwarded to officials at the Alcoman mission.

Weeks later, a mounted contingent of armed soldiers arrived in El Paso, all dressed as monks and leading a pack train. The train carried little of value, but to an observer it resembled the others that traveled the valley road to the north bearing church items and coins. The intent of the soldiers was to invite an attack from Nevarez and his gang, surprise them, and attempt to capture or kill as many as possible.

When one of Chato's scouts reported the approach of the new pack train, Nevarez assembled his men and made preparations to attack it. At a selected point along the trail, the outlaws charged up and out of an arroyo and were among their intended victims within seconds. Much to the surprise and dismay of the brigands, the riders threw back their cloaks, withdrew weapons, and set upon the outlaws.

The fight lasted only minutes and several on each side were killed or wounded. The outlaws, however, had been badly defeated, and those not slain were taken prisoner, roped together, and marched back to Alcoman, hundreds of miles to the south. Among the prisoners was Chato Nevarez.

Months later, Nevarez and his surviving companions were tried in Alcoman, found guilty of robbery and murder, and sentenced to hang. While they awaited their fate on the gallows, the outlaws resided in cramped, filthy, stone-walled cells. Their constant visitors were rats and roaches.

Knowing that such things had been accomplished in the past, Nevarez decided to try to buy his way out of prison. Over a period of time, the outlaw befriended one of the guards and the monk who accompanied him when he brought food to the prisoners. Chato told him many stories of his cache of gold and other riches far to the north in Soledad Canyon. When Nevarez described the treasure and its location to the guard, the monk, unknown to the two men, wrote the information down. Despite his efforts to purchase his freedom, Nevarez, along with his companions, was hung a week later.

The activities of the outlaw Chato Nevarez would likely be relegated to little more than a mere footnote in New Mexico history were it not for an unusual event that occurred in 1930. In July of that year, a man wrestled a very old, heavy, metal safe into an El Paso, Texas, establishment that specialized in refurbishing and repairing such items, along with old trunks, chests, and strongboxes. The owner of the safe explained to the proprietor that the item had come from the old monastery at Alcoman, deep in Mexico, and had been handed down in his family for a number of generations. He left the safe to be restored and made usable.

Days later as he was removing a rusted section of an interior wall of the safe, the proprietor discovered an old document that apparently had been hidden between the inner lining and the outer wall. The document, in longhand, was written in Castilian Spanish and was somewhat beyond the grasp of the proprietor or any of his employees. When the owner of the safe returned, he was given the manuscript along with an explanation of its discovery.

Curious about the contents of the document, the owner of the safe sent it to a Spanish linguist at the University of Texas at Austin who translated it into English. It turned out to be a description of Chato Nevarez's treasure cave in the Organ Mountains as it was written down by the silent monk nearly three centuries earlier.

The translation, in its exact wording, reads:

Go to El Paso del Norte and inquire where the Organ Mountains are. The mountains are located up the river two days travel from El Paso del Norte by horseback. It is a large mountain range with some peaks on it. You will find in these mountains two gaps. One is called Tortuga and the other is called Soledad. Before entering the first gap, turn to your right and go to about the middle of the slope of the mountain where you will find a very thick juniper tree. From this tree, proceed downhill 100 paces to a spot covered with small stones. Look for a blue stone a great deal larger than the others. A cross was made on this stone by a chisel. Remove this slab and dig about a man's height and you will find a hole full of silver taken from the packs of six mules. You will find at the bottom of this hole some boards. Remove the boards and you will find coins from three mule trains we captured and buried there. Following this, go to Soledad Canyon and follow up the pass until you reach a very large spring which is the source of the water which runs through the canyon. The spring is covered with cattails.

Proceed to the right to about the middle of the slope of the mountains. Look with great care for three juniper trees which are very thick and set not very far apart. In front of these trees is a small precipice in which can be found a large, flat rock on which a cross has been carved with a chisel. Between the trees and the rock exists a mine which belonged to a wealthy Spaniard named Jose Colon. The mine is so rich that the silver ore can be cut with a knife. The opening of the mine is covered by a large door we constructed from the timbers of the juniper. On top of this door is placed a large red rock. It will take 25 men to remove this rock. Just inside the door can be found gold crucifixes, images, platters, vases, and other items. Passing this, continue down into the mine shaft and you will encounter a tall stack of silver bars. Beyond this lies mining equipment. Thousands of families will be benefited by this wealth.

This incredible treasure has never been found and is still being searched for today.

Two years after the translation of the document, yet another one containing the description of a treasure hidden by Pedro Nevarez, along with its location, was discovered. It has been concluded that, during the surprise attack by the soldiers on Nevarez and his gang, one of the outlaws managed to escape and hide among the cattails along the bank of the river. Badly wounded and losing blood, the bandit managed to crawl away. Two days later he was found lying near death on the steps of the Doña Ana mission.

Barely clinging to life, the outlaw made his final confession to the priest who attended him. He told the holy man about stealing the golden church items and described where they were hidden in Soledad Canyon. The priest wrote down the words of the dying man as he spoke, careful to include as many details as possible. The next morning, the outlaw was found dead. The priest, viewing the tale of the buried treasure as the incoherent ravings of a dying man, disregarded it and filed it along with other mission paperwork and documents. Other church duties kept him busy and eventually he forgot about it.

In October 1879, the Doña Ana mission was attacked by the Apache war chief Victorio and his band. After killing a number of priests, monks, and Mexican laborers, the Indians ransacked the church, taking the golden and silver icons. Additionally, they raided the nearby storehouses and stole food, guns, and ammunition. Books, letters, and church documents that were encountered were simply scattered and tossed, many of them carried away by the unceasing desert winds.

Among the few documents recovered the following day was the account of the dying outlaw as it had been written down by the priest. In part, it read:

In Soledad Canyon there is a natural cave in the brow of a hill opening toward the south. There is a cross cut into the rock above the entrance to the cave and directly in front of a young juniper tree. For better directions, there are three medium-sized peaks toward the rising sun whose shadows converge in the morning 250 paces east of the cave entrance and a little to the south. Two hundred and fifty paces from this point directly north can be found an embankment from where by looking straight ahead you can see the Jornada del Muerto as far as the eye can see. The distance from this point to the cave should be exactly the same as the distance to the place where the shadows of the peaks converge. One hundred paces from the entrance to the cave down the arroyo you will find a dripping spring. The entrance to the cave has been covered to the depth of a man's height, and ten paces beyond the entrance there is an adobe wall which must be torn down in order to gain access. At the bottom of a long tunnel, the cave separates into two parts: The left cave contains two mule-loads worth of coined silver and the right cave contains candlesticks, images, and crucifixes taken in a robbery.

One day during the autumn of 1913, a sometime miner named Ben Brown was hunting for deer in a remote canyon in a New Mexico mountain range when he made a most serendipitous discovery. Brown spotted a deer browsing among some low-growing shrubs, aimed his rifle, and fired a shot. Unfortunately, Brown only wounded the animal, which bounded away among the rocks. Brown followed the blood-spattered trail for about three hundred yards before finally losing it. Exhausted, he sat down in the shade of a large juniper to catch his breath. As he rested beneath the tree, he scanned the slope below him in hope of finding the wounded deer but spotted something more interesting.

Not too far distant and on the same hillside as Brown reclined, he saw an area that appeared unnatural, one that seemed to have been filled in with rocks. Based on Brown's career as a miner, he recognized immediately that the placement of the rocks was done by men, not nature. Curious, he wondered why anyone would go to so much trouble to relocate several tons of rock.

Brown made his way down to the site and looked around. As he did so, he recalled the old tale often told in the area about the outlaw Chato Nevarez burying a great treasure somewhere in Soledad Canyon. Looking around, Brown noted the three "medium-sized peaks" alluded to in the dying outlaw's account to the priest. From the juniper under which he had sat, Brown paced off 250 steps in the direction of the rising sun, then north for the same distance. When he stopped, he found himself on a low ridge from which he had a grand view of the Jornada del Muerto, the so-called Route of the Dead Man, a vast, arid plain that extended as far as the eye could see and that had claimed the lives of so many travelers in the past. Returning to the juniper tree, Brown paced off one hundred steps downhill and stopped in an arroyo where the outlaw said a dripping spring was located. Though he searched for several minutes, he could find no evidence of one. Intuitively, however, he dug into the soft sand that composed the floor of the arroyo and found water seeping in from only eight inches below.

Early the next morning before sunrise, Brown returned to the canyon with an armload of digging tools. He found a comfortable position among the rocks and waited as the sun rose over the peaks behind him. As it did, he watched the progress of shadows across the landscape before him, and around midmorning he noted the spot where the shadows of the three peaks converged. He walked to the location and marked it with a cairn of rocks. From this point, he walked 250 paces to the west. Here, he found what he was convinced was tons of rock brought in from an adjacent slope to fill a cave. Based on what he recalled from the legend of Chato's treasure, Brown was beginning to believe he had found where it was hidden.

Over the next several days, Brown undertook the task of removing the rock fill from the vertical entrance to the cave. Working alone, he hauled away tons of debris, exposing the opening to a cave. By the time he had removed six feet of the rock, he found himself standing on a large flat stone, one that had clearly been wedged into its present position by men. Scraping away dust and gravel, Brown exposed the image of a crucifix on the surface of the stone, one that had been scratched into the rock with a chisel.

Brown was discouraged by the slow progress he was making and the grueling work involved with the excavation. He covered the flat rock with brush and debris and returned to his home in Las Cruces. The following morning, he walked into the county clerk's office and filed a mining claim on the location in Soledad Canyon. From there, he drove to a hardware store and purchased a pickup load of camping gear and more digging tools, then returned to the cave. He drove as close as he could to

It's likely that a great treasure remains to be found in a cave in the mountains outside of Las Cruces, New Mexico. Library of Congress

the excavation site, then, making several trips, carried his gear the rest of the way and set up a temporary camp. He cut down what he considered to be the identifying juniper tree in case anybody else might be searching for the lost treasure of Chato Nevarez.

Though it took most of two days, Brown, wielding a heavy sledge hammer, broke up the flat rock bearing the etched image of a crucifix and removed the pieces. To his frustration, he discovered that the cave below the stone had also been filled with rock and soil.

For the next two weeks, Brown lowered himself into the slowly deepening excavation, removing the fill one bucketful at a time. When he reached a depth of twelve feet, he observed that the shaft gradually began leveling out. It was also much narrower than the entrance, forcing Brown to crawl on his hands and knees during the excavation process. More time passed, and several more tons of debris were removed. Just as Brown was beginning to think the project was becoming hopeless, he found a gold Spanish coin lying on the floor of the cave. It bore a date of 1635. The discovery provided Brown with a reason to continue.

Finally, Brown came to the adobe wall he recalled from the legend. Wielding a heavy crowbar in the cramped space, he succeeded in tearing it down. Beyond, Brown found the cave was clear for another ten yards. He crawled through it and came to a chamber large enough for him to stand upright. Beyond the chamber and in the light of his torch, he saw where the cave continued. Hurrying over to it, he was disappointed to find that it, too, had been filled with gravel and soil.

The patient Brown continued with the excavation of the cave. One day, he dug out an ancient pickaxe from the debris. Later, he shipped it to an acquaintance who worked at the Chicago Field Museum of Natural History and requested an identification. Brown subsequently learned the tool was made of hand-forged metal and the casting process suggested it was probably manufactured in Spain sometime during the sixteenth century. Heartened, Brown continued his back-breaking labor in the cave.

From time to time, Brown was forced to abandon digging at the treasure site to look in on his own mining operations at other locations in the region. He also began taking a week off from the heavy labor now and then to rest his aching body. For over a year he continued the slow, painstaking process of removing the dirt fill from the cave, one bucketful at a time. Weeks would pass and he would grow discouraged, only to find another artifact among the debris that would give him hope that the treasure was not far beyond.

Brown's difficulties were to grow worse. His other mines were not particularly productive and he began losing money. Eventually, he was forced to close down these operations and take jobs in and around Las Cruces in order to provide an income for himself and his family. For several years while he worked off and on in the cave, Brown was employed at other mining operations and sometimes worked as a forest ranger. He even made extra money as a musician on weekends.

Twenty years elapsed and Brown was still excavating dirt from the cave. At one point during his work, he sought some advice from a college professor named Arturo Campa who taught at the University of Denver and was regarded as an authority on tales and legends of lost treasure in the New Mexico Southwest. As it turned out, Campa was keenly interested in the amazing legend of Chato Nevarez. Brown told Campa of his discovery and his two-decades-long attempt to remove the fill from the cave. Much to Campa's surprise, Brown told him that the cave was not in the Soledad Canyon in the Organ Mountains, but rather in a canyon bearing the same name in the Doña Ana range some fifteen miles to the west.

Intrigued, Campa asked to be taken to the excavation and Brown readily agreed. Of the site, Campa wrote:

> The tunnel against the hillside had the appearance of a natural cave, very similar to the subterranean formations associated with Carlsbad Caverns, except there was no moisture and the floor was covered with topsoil. For a short distance we walked upright; then we stopped and began crawling on all fours. About 200 feet down into the earth we came upon a point where the cave split into a Y going in two directions. I took one side and Ben followed the other. This was as far as he had cleared but I could see the passage continued indefinitely. Back at the surface, Ben pointed out the landmarks of the three peaks, the jornada, and the spring.

Brown explained to Campa that he was trying to obtain financial backing in order to purchase some expensive equipment that would facilitate the excavation process. Though he approached a number of potential investors, he was never able to secure the money he needed. Around this same time, several other mines he had an interest in were growing more productive, had begun some profit, and required his attention. He spent less and less time at the cave.

One day, about two years following his visit to the excavation, Professor Campa received a letter from Ben Brown, one that conveyed a great deal of excitement relative to the excavation project. In the letter, Brown invited Campa back to the site so he could show him what he had discovered. He didn't want to take the chance, he wrote, of describing what he found in the letter for fear that it would fall into the wrong hands. Because of a number of university obligations he was saddled with at the time, Campa was not free to travel. Four months later, he learned that Ben Brown had died.

Subsequent investigations, along with a search through his personal belongings, revealed that Brown had never left a map showing the location of the cave. Furthermore, he apparently had never told his wife and children of his discovery. As far as is known, the only person he shared the information with was Professor Campa, and Campa passed away not long afterward. Whatever Ben Brown discovered in Chato Nevarez's treasure cave may never be known.

Did Brown penetrate the rock and soil fill in the cave to the treasure of golden church artifacts and silver coins? And if so, what did he do with them, if anything? Since Brown left little to his family other than his mining interests, it is likely that the treasure is still hidden deep inside the cave Brown spent over two decades excavating. Whatever the truth of the matter, Ben Brown carried it with him to his grave.

JEAN LAFFITE'S GALVESTON TREASURE

Who hasn't thrilled to tales of swashbuckling pirates as they sailed the seven seas in search of adventure and treasure? Pirate novels and movies have captivated the attention of and entertained millions over the years, and several of these outlaws of the open ocean are as well known as many of the land-based banditti. The pirate Blackbeard, a subject of fascinating legend and lore, raided and looted all along the Atlantic coast of the United States until finally captured and executed. The colorful Jean Laffite was the most notorious brigand to ply the waters of the Gulf of Mexico, even attracting the attention of the United States Navy. Like Blackbeard, Laffite is often associated with tales of buried treasure, and there exists compelling evidence that one of the greatest caches of this colorful pirate is still buried near the city of Galveston.

For years, the name Laffite struck fear in the hearts of captains of merchant and passenger vessels that traveled along the Texas and Louisiana coasts. From his base of operations in New Orleans, Laffite commanded a fleet of several warships that ranged out into the Gulf of Mexico preying on unarmed passenger and trade vessels. In the process, Laffite and his pirates accumulated millions of dollars worth of gold and silver ingots, gold coin, and jewelry. For years, not a single ship sailing gulf waters was safe from the depredations of Laffite's marauders. In response to this ongoing threat, the United States Navy was finally called in to patrol these waters and offer protection to shippers and travelers alike.

So great was the pressure placed on Laffite by the Navy that he was eventually forced to abandon his Louisiana stronghold, leading his fleet westward along the coast and eventually arriving at Galveston Island. On landing, Laffite soon discovered that the island was already being used as a headquarters by a rival pirate. Since Laffite's forces were three times as great as his competitor, he simply drove him from the site and claimed it for himself. Laffite and his men moved into an abandoned Spanish fortress, the remains of which can still be viewed just west of the Galveston Yacht Basin.

From Galveston Island, Laffite ranged out across the gulf and preyed primarily on the Spanish ships transporting gold and silver from Mexico to Spain on the other side of the Atlantic Ocean.

It wasn't long before the U.S. Navy learned that Laffite was still a major threat to ships. Though bothered by the pirate's arrogant snubbing of U.S. authority, government officials decided not to pursue him as long as he was preying on Spanish ships, preferring to let Spanish authorities protect their own vessels.

Laffite, however, was an opportunist, and, when the chance to seize an American ship presented itself, he took it. When it became clear that the pirate was back in business attacking American vessels, the navy once again went in pursuit of the sea bandit, this time sending the USS *Interprise* into the gulf to confront him.

The *Interprise*, commanded by Captain Kearney, an experienced officer, sailed directly to Galveston Island to force a showdown with Laffite. Flying a flag of truce, Kearney steered the *Interprise* right up to the island and entered into negotiations with Laffite. Kearney invited the pirate to cease his operations in American territory and quit preying on American passenger and merchant ships. Laffite admitted to Kearney that, against his own orders, two of his captains had indeed attacked American ships. Laffite sent a contingent of his men to locate the two officers and return with them. When they arrived, the pirate leader had them hung in front of Kearney in hope of appeasing the captain.

Kearney, however, was not impressed. On returning to the *Interprise*, he had the ship's cannons aimed at Laffite's headquarters, then sent a message to the pirate stating he had exactly thirty days to vacate the island. If the pirates were not gone after the appointed time, he stated, the *Interprise's* artillery would destroy the fortress and all of the ships in the harbor, and survivors would be taken prisoner.

For three weeks it appeared that Lafitte had no intention of abandoning the island. At the beginning of the fourth week, however, he ordered his crew to begin loading several chests, casks, and leather sacks, all presumably filled with his treasures, the ill-gotten gains of numerous raids, onto a small ship called the *Pride*. This done, the *Pride* was observed sailing northward into Galveston Bay and then westward into the Clear Creek estuary. After sailing a short distance up the creek, the water became too shallow to accommodate the *Pride's* draft, so Laffite had the treasure off-loaded into rowboats. The rowboats, each with a pair of stout sailors at the oars, continued upriver for another half-hour before turning toward shore. At a point determined by Laffite, the immense pirate treasure was buried in approximately two dozen different locations along the banks overlooking Clear Creek.

After returning to the *Pride*, Laffite found it had become mired in the bottom sands of the channel during his absence. The pirate crew worked for most of the rest of the day to free the ship from the sandy grip, but to no avail. Finally, he simply abandoned it and returned to the fortress on Galveston Island.

During the next few days, the crew of the *Interprise* observed the pirates transporting goods from the fortress onto the ships anchored in the harbor. Before the thirty-day limit imposed by Kearney was out, Laffite, commanding the lead ship, led his fleet out of the bay and into the open waters of the Gulf of Mexico. Before leaving, Laffite ordered the fortress burned, presumably so no one else could use it. For reasons unknown, he abandoned about two dozen of his crewmen on the island.

The pirate Laffite never returned to Clear Creek to recover what must have amounted to several millions of dollars worth of treasure in gold, silver, and jewels. Weeks later, after Captain Kearney filed his report,

"Pirate's Alley" in New Orleans, Jean Laffite's base of operations when he wasn't marauding in the Gulf of Mexico. Library of Congress

a number of expeditions were undertaken by various groups of treasure hunters to try to locate Laffite's incredible cache, but none knew where to look. The only information available stated simply that the pirate fortune was transported some distance up Clear Creek and buried.

Several decades after Lafitte's abandonment of Galveston Island, the city of Galveston grew and prospered as an important Texas Gulf coast port. As with many such towns associated with seagoing commerce, Galveston attracted a number of broken down gobs who, for one reason or another, were no longer able to hold jobs on the sailing vessels. Living in shacks and flophouses, these old sailors frequented the many taverns that could be found in Galveston's port side of town. Among these old-timers was a grizzled sea veteran known to the locals only as Crazy Ben. Ben was like most of the drifters and derelicts that hung around the bars telling stories of their days on the open ocean. The principal thing that distinguished Crazy Ben from his companions, however, was the fact that he paid for his meals and drinks with Spanish gold coins.

For years, Ben refused to reveal the source of his coins, but late one evening when he had had too much to drink, he told an interested listener an amazing story about finding a lost pirate treasure. It was a story that was to cost him his life.

When he was but a boy, Crazy Ben had a job as a cabin boy to none other than the pirate Jean Lafitte himself. While Ben was not a member of the group that rowed the casks and chests of treasure up Clear Creek and buried them, he knew all about it, having watched from the deck of the *Pride* as the crewmen loaded the wealth in gold coins and bars and jewelry into the lifeboats and rowed away. He was also, he claimed, among the group that was abandoned on Galveston Island when Laffite and his fleet sailed away. After making his way to the mainland, Ben earned his living working on area farms, swabbing out saloons, and getting an odd job here and there. During this time, he kept searching for Laffite's buried treasure.

Then one day he found it, or at least part of it. While digging along the bank of Clear Creek not far from the present-day community of Nassau Bay, the tip of Crazy Ben's shovel struck the top of one of the wooden casks. With difficulty, he raised the heavy object part of the way out of the hole, smashed open the lid, and discovered hundreds of Spanish gold coins within, the same coins he used to pay for his meals and drinks. After placing several of the coins in his pockets, Ben reburied the cask, returning to it from time to time when he ran out of money.

Ben's practice of retrieving a few coins from the cask continued for many years, and during that time men who had observed him spend freely at the taverns had attempted to follow him when he journeyed up the trail that paralleled Clear Creek. Ben always suspected he was being followed, so he took a route that enabled him to elude his trackers.

One evening in a Galveston Island tavern, Ben, as usual, had had too much to drink and talked too long and too loud about his buried cask of gold coins. As a result, he aroused the interest of a group of newcomers at a nearby table, some out-of-work seamen who were down on their luck and needing some money. During the early morning hours when the tavern was closing down, Crazy Ben staggered out of the saloon and into the street and slowly made his way to his poor living quarters near the bay. Only a few yards behind him followed the seamen who overheard his conversation.

Since Crazy Ben did not carry much money on his person, it is presumed that the men who followed him were intent on learning the location of his gold-filled cask. What they found out from Ben will never be known, however, for the next morning his body was found floating in the shallow waters of the bay, his throat slashed.

Following the murder of Crazy Ben, none of the Spanish gold coins ever appeared in circulation again and it is presumed by many that he took the secret location of the treasure to his grave.

Though never substantiated, rumors have circulated around Galveston since the 1950s that now and then individual Spanish gold coins were occasionally found on the banks of Clear Creek not far from Nassau Bay. It is probable that, if true, these coins may have been spilled by Crazy Ben during one of his retrievals.

What Crazy Ben found was only a small portion of the large treasure buried by Jean Lafitte and his pirates. The remaining chests, casks, and leather pouches filled with gold, silver, and jewels undoubtedly still lie buried somewhere along the bank next to Clear Creek. Experts can only guess at the value of such a treasure, but most agree it would be worth several hundred million dollars today.

OUTLAW PLUMMER'S LOST GOLD

In the annals of Montana history, no single outlaw approaches the notoriety and repute accorded Henry Plummer. The western part of this magnificent state is steeped in the legend and lore of this colorful and infamous criminal, and the stories of his buried treasures have lured hundreds of fortune hunters from the rest of the country in search of them. A few have been found, but the majority of Plummer's buried treasures remain lost, still tempting and luring the hopeful as they have been for one hundred years.

As notorious as Plummer was, and as much newspaper space as has been devoted to his nefarious activities, his background prior to arriving in the American West is unknown. Many are convinced he came from somewhere in the East, that he was a man of education and distinction, and it has been written that he often conducted himself as a refined and cultured gentleman. On arriving in the region of the Rocky Mountains, however, Plummer learned quickly that fortunes could more easily be made through robbery and murder than by hard work, and he thereafter devoted himself to the business of taking other people's money and gold via unlawful and despicable acts.

Plummer led a varied life during his time in the West. Though known primarily as an outlaw, he was also a successful gambler for a time, and even a lawman. Eventually, however, he came to be known as "The Scourge of the Rockies," and history suggests that he stole more money and gold than any other famous outlaw of the American West.

It is believed that Plummer first landed in Nevada when he came West; at least, that is where his story begins. As a result of his implication in a number of illegal activities there, mostly robbery, he was run out of the state by law enforcement authorities. He fled to California where he found the pickings much easier, and for the next year or so he robbed miners of their hard-earned gold until officials there began making things hot for him. Just barely one step ahead of the law, Plummer escaped to Washington state where he set himself up as a gambler.

Plummer became very successful running a poker table in Walla Walla; so successful, in fact, that many of those who lost suspected him of running a crooked game. Though he was never caught cheating, Plummer closed down his game and moved on to other activities. It was said that he missed the adventure and excitement associated with robbing miners, travelers, and stagecoaches. Some historians even suggest Plummer took a perverse joy in being pursued by lawmen and that gambling never held the same thrill for him.

As Plummer was contemplating a return to the gold fields of California, he got into trouble in Walla Walla. Some say a woman was involved, but whatever the reason, he was run out of town. Weeks later, he rode into Lewiston, Idaho, and decided to remain for a while.

At Lewiston, Plummer encountered a number of men, all thieves and murderers, that he believed would comprise an efficient and effective gang. Within a short span of time, they were aggressively robbing stagecoaches, freight wagons, miners, and travelers, often killing their victims so they would never be able to identify the perpetrators. In a matter of just a few months, the Plummer Gang amassed an impressive fortune in gold ingots, coins, and nuggets. From the first successful robbery, the gang was constantly pursued by lawmen.

One of Plummer's gang members was a man named Jack Cleveland. Cleveland was a constant thorn in the side of Plummer, but because he was a fearless robber and a ruthless killer, the leader liked having him in the gang. Once, in a fit of drunken rage, Cleveland got into an argument with a fellow gang member over a petty matter and shot the man down in cold blood. Some claim that Plummer lived in fear of Cleveland and that he suspected the man would eventually cause trouble.

As the number of lawmen chasing the Plummer Gang increased, the outlaws were having difficulty staying out of their reach. A major problem associated with fleeing from pursuers was related to the fact that Plummer insisted on transporting his huge load of stolen gold ingots, coins, and nuggets by mule wherever he went instead of caching the hoard somewhere. In time, Plummer's personal mule train of riches had grown to four animals, and because the overburdened and sometimes recalcitrant animals made escape difficult, the outlaws often found themselves overtaken by pursuers and forced into shootouts. The gang members constantly complained about the pack animals to the outlaw leader, but Plummer ignored them, reminding them that he was in charge. At one point, Cleveland threatened to shoot the mules if Plummer didn't come up with a better plan of taking care of the booty. It was estimated that Plummer's fortune during this time was worth well over a million dollars.

Successful robberies became more and more difficult and Plummer and his gang members had become all too well known to lawmen and citizens throughout much of northern Idaho. Because they were recognized everywhere they traveled in the area, Plummer decided they needed to move their operation to someplace else. He selected Montana.

During the autumn of 1862, the Plummer Gang arrived in the tiny settlement of Sun River, Montana, about twenty miles east of Great Falls. The outlaws liked what they found in the area and decided it would serve as a suitable base of operations. The outlaws moved into an abandoned ranch house that Plummer found a short distance out of town. Once the outlaws settled in, Plummer counted out amounts of gold from the treasure carried by the mules and paid each member of the gang, keeping the largest portion for himself. The outlaws grew upset and told Plummer they were under the impression that all of the gold was to be split equally among them, making each of them wealthy men. Plummer, however, explained to them that, as leader of the gang, the gold was his and the men were only working for him and paid accordingly.

The most vocal dissenter was Cleveland, who insisted he stole more of the gold than Plummer, thus at least half of it should be his. Though furious, Cleveland, along with the other gang members, settled for the small payment offered by Plummer, but none was happy about it.

After the gang had been in Sun River for several weeks, Plummer informed them that he was going to travel to the gold fields near the town of Bannock, Idaho, in order to determine if the area would be suitable to carry out more robberies. As Plummer was loading the gold onto the mules, several of the gang members approached and informed him they didn't like the idea of him riding away with all of the loot. As a compromise, Plummer agreed to let one of the gang members accompany him to Bannock. The men chose Cleveland.

During the trip, Plummer and Cleveland rarely spoke, their animosity for each other apparent. Plummer was convinced Cleveland planned to kill him and take all of the gold for himself. As a result, he got little sleep and was irritable and nervous the entire time they were in Bannock. Nothing was accomplished, and the two men, along with the four mules transporting well over a million dollars in gold, returned to Sun River.

When the two outlaws arrived at the hideout, they discovered the other gang members had ridden into Great Falls, some twenty miles to the west, for some drinking and gambling. When Cleveland went into the house, Plummer unloaded the gold from the four mules, unsaddled and unbridled the animals, and turned them out into the pasture. Plummer then went into the house and poured a drink for himself and for Cleveland.

As the two men played cards, Plummer made certain that Cleveland's glass was always filled with whiskey, while he himself only pretended to drink. After about two hours, Cleveland was drunk and passed out at the table. While he was asleep, Plummer carried the packs of gold down to a nearby small creek, some two hundred yards from the ranch house, and buried them.

The next morning when the two men awoke, Plummer told Cleveland that he was going to ride back to Bannock to re-evaluate the possibilities of conducting some robberies. Cleveland insisted he was going along and saddled his horse. When Plummer rode up a few minutes later ready to depart but without the pack-laden mules, Cleveland asked him where the gold was. Plummer told the outlaw that he had hidden it in a safe place. Enraged, Cleveland pulled a revolver, leveled it at Plummer, and threatened to kill him. An instant later, Plummer drew his own weapon from his holster and shot Cleveland, killing him instantly. Without a second look at the dead outlaw, Plummer spurred his horse past the body of Cleveland and rode on to Bannock.

After spending a few days in the Idaho town, Plummer discovered that the opportunities to amass a fortune by stealing were great. While he made plans to accumulate more gold and add to his already immense fortune, Plummer ingratiated himself with local businessmen and politicians. Weeks later, in May 1863, he somehow managed to get elected sheriff of Bannock. Shortly after taking office, Plummer returned to Sun River and met with his gang members. He made each of them deputies and they returned with him to Bannock. Days later, Plummer returned to Sun River, and courted and married a woman named Electa Bryan. The two of them traveled to Bannock and moved into a small frame house in town. Many years later when she was an elderly woman, Electa told a newspaper reporter that Plummer told her about his large fortune in gold ingots, nuggets, and coins he had buried next to the small creek at Sun River, and that he had never had an opportunity to return to the area to retrieve it.

Plummer, as sheriff, along with his deputized gang members, used his position to steal and confiscate gold from the many miners and freight companies in the area. If anyone opposed him, Plummer either had them killed or killed them himself. During the short six-month period Plummer was sheriff of Bannock, he and his men were responsible for 102 murders and uncountable robberies.

As had become his custom, Plummer loaded the stolen gold onto mules and led them everywhere he traveled. When the packs were full, Plummer, alone, led the mules to some remote location near Bannock, unloaded the gold, and buried it. Plummer never told anyone where he had hidden his gold and, as far as anyone knows, never left a map or directions indicating the location of his many caches.

In addition to the huge cache near the small stream that flowed close to the ranch house at Sun River, Plummer is known to have cached over $200,000 near Birdtail Rock on the Mullan Road during the time he returned to Sun River to marry Electa. A short time after his wedding, Plummer and his gang held up a stagecoach near Deer Lodge, Montana, took $50,000 worth of gold, and buried it within hours somewhere along the bank of Cottonwood Creek. Near Cascade, a few miles south of Sun River, Plummer reportedly buried $300,000 in gold not far from the old St. Peter's mission. History records the outlaw was hanged before he could return to this cache as well as several others. According to Electa, none of the caches were ever retrieved by the outlaw.

It did not take long for the businessmen and citizens of Bannock to grow weary of Plummer's reign of terror and theft. Secret meetings were held by the townsfolk who discussed ways to rid themselves of Plummer and his gang. A vigilante committee was organized and armed, and their charge was to rid the region of Plummer and his influence. One at a time, individual members of the gang were tracked down, apprehended, and hung. Others, realizing their days were numbered, fled from Bannock, never to return. On January 10, 1864, the vigilantes caught up with Plummer, and with little fanfare hung him, bringing to an end his vicious depredations throughout the region.

Some who have studied the life and times of Henry Plummer have suggested that a number of the townsfolk of Bannock were jealous of the outlaw's success and coveted his great wealth, and that in eliminating him they might somehow come into possession of the vast amount of gold he was known to possess. The vigilantes, many have maintained, were little better than the gang of outlaws led by Plummer. A number of eyewitnesses have reported that, prior to hanging him, several of the vigilantes forced Plummer to reveal the location of at least one of his gold caches. Whether this is true or not is unknown, but it is a fact that a few members of the vigilante committee became wealthy only a few days following Plummer's execution.

In 1869, Electa Plummer returned to Sun River with a map that reputedly showed the location of the massive fortune in gold ingots, nuggets, and coins buried by her late husband. The map, she claimed, had been drawn by one of the gang members. Though she searched for days, she was unable to locate the treasure. Many who knew her were convinced she was unable to interpret the rather cryptic map she carried and thus she searched in the wrong places.

A stepson of one of the surviving Plummer Gang members was twelve years old in 1875 when he was playing along a shallow creek not far from the old Sun River ranch house used by the gang members. The stepson, whose name was Henry Ford, was digging in the soft soil of the bank next to the stream and, to his great surprise, unearthed several old leather sacks filled with small gold ingots. He dragged one of the sacks home and showed his stepfather, who recognized the ingots and estimated their value at around $60,000. Several days later, the stepfather asked Henry to lead him back to the location where he found the gold bars. The two returned to the area but were unable to relocate the hole Henry had excavated. Though they searched the area for hours, they were unable to find anything.

In 1890, a man named Jack Young arrived at Sun River. His mother, he claimed, was the sister to one of the gang members. She was in the possession of a crudely drawn map which she claimed showed where Henry Plummer buried his huge gold cache near the creek. She turned the map over to Jack, and, following it, he came to a location not far from where Henry Ford found the leather sack filled with gold ingots fourteen years earlier. After several minutes of digging into the soil of the creek bank, Jack Young uncovered more leather sacks filled with gold ingots.

These are the only recorded instances of any of Plummer's loot being recovered. Though substantial, the sacks of gold ingots found near Sun River represented only a fraction of the wealth the outlaw buried at or near this location, and most researchers are convinced the bulk of the fortune still lies buried nearby.

In addition to this site, it has been estimated that Plummer buried the loot from other robberies in as many as six other locations throughout Idaho and Montana, locations treasure hunters are still searching for.

THE SAM BASS TREASURE

Few outlaws in America's history have captivated the public imagination as has Sam Bass. Yet, this bad man's personality and bandit activities have long remained shrouded in mystery. Mystery also reigns supreme when it comes to Bass's buried wealth, a fortune in accumulated gold coins and jewelry taken during stagecoach holdups and train robberies. There is a preponderance of evidence that Bass's cache was buried in Denton or Williamson County, Texas, and some of it has even been found. The remainder, estimated to be worth hundreds of thousands of dollars today, still lies hidden only inches below the surface and is tempting, ever tempting those who continue to search for it.

Biographies of the outlaw Sam Bass generally consist of a mixture of fact and legend. According to the old folk song, *The Ballad of Sam Bass*, he gained the reputation as a Robin Hood kind of figure who stole money from the rich and gave it all to the poor. Even so, there remain plenty of facts about his escapades that provide credence to his reputation as an efficient and cunning outlaw and shrewd and successful robber.

According to research, Sam Bass was born in 1851 in Indiana. He was orphaned at a very young age and passed around to various relatives and forced to work long, hard hours on the farms where he lived. When he wasn't in the fields, he was in the woods cutting, splitting, and hauling firewood.

When he turned eighteen, Bass decided he had had enough of the toil and tedium of farm work and determined to seek greater adventures far beyond the western horizon. For years, he heard travelers relate tales of Texas, cowboys, gunfighters, and working as cowhands on large ranches. The lure of adventure and romance was too strong to resist much longer, and one day Bass packed his few belongings and headed out on foot for the Lone Star State.

Sam Bass arrived in Denton County in 1870. He turned nineteen years of age during his long trek in a lonely trailside camp with no one to help him celebrate. Bass was a strapping young man who was eager and willing to work, and before long he found a job on a nearby ranch. While the young man was digging postholes, building fences, and cleaning barns, he was also learning the fundamentals of horsemanship and livestock handling and was soon given greater responsibilities.

For months, this Indiana youth was excited about being a working cow hand. He spent hours in the saddle riding, roping, tending livestock, and performing other ranch-related chores, but as before, he soon grew bored and sought more creative and satisfying outlets for his energies.

Bass soon obtained a job with a Denton freight company owned and operated by the county sheriff. He was assigned to hauling freight throughout much of North Texas, and in the process became intimate with the countryside, the trails, and the people who lived there. Bass was a handsome, charming young man, and made friends easily.

Around this time, Bass became keenly interested in horse racing, often squandering his meager pay betting at local competitions. He managed to save some money, however, and in time purchased a racing mare and began traveling around the region betting on his horse against others. Success came fast, and Bass extended his operations throughout much of north Texas and into Oklahoma, racing his mare at every opportunity. The mare was successful, and Bass's winnings grew.

After several months of racing, Bass encountered Joel Collins, a friend from his ranching days. Collins convinced Bass to invest his sizeable poke into a cattle herd he learned was up for sale. Collins then combined his own herd with his friend's new one, and together they made arrangements to drive them to Dodge City, Kansas, where they expected to sell them and make a lot of money.

By the time Bass and Collins had delivered their herd to Dodge City, however, the bottom had fallen out of the cattle market and they stood to lose a lot of money if they sold. They decided to wait for a few days before deciding what to do. While playing cards at a Dodge City tavern, the two men overheard a conversation about some big money being paid for beef in Deadwood, Dakota Territory, some 450 miles to the north as the crow flies. At the time, Deadwood was in the middle of a mining boom, and miners and citizens were paying top dollar for fresh meat. Weeks later, the two men drove the herd into Deadwood where it was sold at a good profit.

Bass and Collins paid off their drovers and other expenses and found their pockets still heavy with gold coins. They decided to celebrate their good fortune, went to a tavern, and bought drinks for everyone. The party went on into the night and the following morning and included a great deal of imbibing and gambling. By the time the sun rose, Bass and Collins discovered they'd spent nearly all of the money they earned from the sale of their cattle. Nearly broke, dispirited, and disgusted with themselves, the two men wondered how they could ever afford to return to Texas.

For several days, they searched for work in Deadwood but to no avail. What little money they had left was spent on food and a hotel room, but that didn't last long. Desperate, the two men decided to rob a stagecoach. Enlisting the help of three friends they made in town, Bass and Collins stopped a coach several miles out of town and relieved the passengers of their money and valuables. It was so easy, and the take was so impressive, that the men decided this would be their new career. For the next six weeks they held up several stagecoaches within only a few miles of Deadwood.

As with his other pursuits, Bass eventually grew bored with robbing stages. He searched about for greater challenges. He considered holding up the Deadwood bank, but after a cursory inspection decided that the heavy security would have made it much too difficult. Gradually, the Bass gang drifted south searching for other targets. They robbed more stagecoaches along the way, and eventually ended up in Big Springs, Nebraska.

Here, Bass discovered, the Union Pacific Railroad ran through town. This was the challenge he sought, the outlaw decided, and he made plans to rob it. One evening, the gang hid in a grove of trees a short distance from the train station. Before long, the eastbound train arrived, and while the crew was distracted with filling the water tanks, the outlaws struck.

After covering their faces with bandannas, the outlaws rode up to the train crew, pointed revolvers at them, and ordered them to unlock the door of the express car. This done, they climbed into the car to find a wooden payroll trunk containing three thousand freshly minted twenty-dollar gold pieces, each bearing a date of 1877. After placing the gold coins in canvas bags and tying them onto their horses, the gang then robbed each of the passengers, taking money, watches, rings, and other jewelry, all of which filled several more sacks. Following this, they mounted up and rode away into the night.

After Bass and his gang had ridden for almost an hour, they stopped to divide up the loot, with Bass, the leader, taking the largest percentage. After this, Bass suggested they split up to confuse pursuers. Within seconds, each of the outlaws was riding away in a different direction.

Weeks later Bass arrived in Texas, his saddlebags bulging with his newfound wealth in gold coins and jewelry. After he had been in Denton for a few days, he learned that his friend Joel Collins had been captured by a posse in Nebraska. When Collins decided to fight it out with his captors, he was shot and killed. When officials examined the contents of Collins's saddlebags, they found over $25,000 in gold and jewelry, all of which was returned to Union Pacific.

Word of the train robbery at Big Springs, Nebraska, eventually reached Denton, and a description of the coins taken was circulated. Because of the newness of the gold pieces and the fact that each bore an 1877 mint date, Bass was afraid to spend any lest they be identified and connect him to the train robbery. He decided instead to cache them in a safe and remote location, intending to return for them at some future date when detection would be less likely.

Bass established a hideout at Cove Hollow, an isolated area sufficiently removed from Denton and surrounded by dense forest and brush. In the hollow, Bass buried the gold coins and jewelry from the Big Springs robbery at a number of different locations.

In a short time, Bass organized another gang for the specific purpose of robbing stagecoaches in the Denton area. Following each robbery, Bass returned to Cove Hollow with his loot and buried it. As before, he cached his accumulating wealth in a number of different locations.

As Bass and his gang became more successful, the stage companies grew more wary, adding more guards. When he realized robbing stages wasn't going to be as easy any longer, Bass turned again to trains. Within six weeks, the Bass gang robbed four trains within a few miles of Denton. During one of the robberies, Bass was recognized, and his image soon appeared on wanted posters throughout the region.

The Texas Rangers were given the responsibility of capturing or killing Sam Bass and breaking up the string of robberies in and around Denton County. As they began closing in, Bass abandoned his Cove Hollow hideout and led his gang southward into Central Texas. When he fled, Bass left his buried loot in Cove Hollow where he believed it would be safe until his return.

Once in Central Texas, Bass made preparations to rob the Williamson County Bank at Round Rock. Unknown to him, one of the gang members, James Murphey, tipped off the Texas Rangers to the plan. The Rangers rode into Round Rock under cover of night hours before the planned robbery and set up a trap.

As Bass and two of his men rode up to the bank, at least two dozen Rangers opened fire and a brief gun battle ensued. One of the gang members was killed during the first few seconds of the fusillade, and Bass was seriously wounded and knocked from his horse. With difficulty, he managed to climb back into the saddle and flee. Miraculously, the third outlaw escaped unharmed.

The Rangers tracked the wounded and badly bleeding Bass. Hours after the robbery, they found him sitting under a big cottonwood tree on the bank of the nearby river. He had lost a great deal of blood and it was clear he was dying. The Rangers tied Bass to his horse and returned him to town. A short time later he died. It was his twenty-seventh birthday.

With the death of the outlaw Sam Bass, people grew curious about the great wealth they believed he had accumulated and buried. Some who were in sympathy with the outlaw insisted he gave his money away to the poor and needy. While there are a few examples of Bass providing some money for the underprivileged, this Robin Hood image was largely concocted and accounts for very little of his fortune. A few others claim Bass gambled and drank away the majority of his wealth, leaving little left to bury. Most people, however, are convinced Bass hid this gold and other loot somewhere in and around Cove Hollow.

During the first decade of the twentieth century, a Texas farmer named Henry Chapman found what many are convinced was a portion of the Sam Bass treasure. Chapman owned a small farm near Springtown in Williamson County. One day while he was riding his mule through the woods between Salt Creek and Clear Fork Creek, Chapman's mount began fighting the bit and attempting to buck its rider. After dismounting to examine the bridle and tighten the girth, Chapman noticed a small mound of dirt just a few feet off the trail. Initially, he thought it was a grave, but on closer inspection he saw that it was something else altogether.

Chapman dug into the mound and was surprised to find a wooden bushel-sized box filled to the top with gold and silver coins. Each of the gold coins bore the date 1877, and the location of the cache was very close to Cove Hollow.

Except for this single discovery, none of the rest of Sam Bass's outlaw loot ever appeared in circulation, supporting the contention that the rest of his treasure remains buried somewhere in Williamson County.

BLACK JACK CHRISTIAN'S
LOST TRAIN ROBBERY GOLD

Black Jack Christian was a small-time outlaw who preyed on travelers and small business enterprises in tiny, out-of-the-way towns in New Mexico and Arizona. Christian never pulled off a significant robbery until November 6, 1897, when he and his partners stole $100,000 in gold and silver coins from a train, along with an untold amount of money, watches, and jewelry taken from the passengers. The gold, buried at a location deep in New Mexico's lava beds near the city of Grants, has never been found.

Just as the sun was setting on the crisp November evening, the scheduled Santa Fe passenger train pulled into the station at Grants, New Mexico. Henry Abel, the fireman, was delighted with the successful trip and looking forward to some time off. As soon as the train came to a stop, he jumped down from the cab of the engine to the loading dock to begin his inspection of the locomotive when Black Jack Christian and his two accomplices stepped out from behind the water tower, masks over their faces and revolvers drawn. As Christian approached Abel, the other two outlaws raced toward the passenger coaches.

Pointing his revolver at Abel's head, Christian ordered him back into the engine. As the two men climbed into the cab, gunfire erupted from the direction of the coaches and Abel knew his worst fears were being realized—the train was being robbed.

As the two outlaws in the cars went from passenger to passenger demanding they place their money, jewelry, and watches into a large canvas sack, Christian ordered the fireman to pull the train about one mile farther up the track. Several minutes later when the train was halted, Christian had the baggage and mail cars detached, then directed Abel to pull the train, now composed of the engine, the passenger cars, and the express car, forward for another mile. When the train was stopped this time, the gas lights of Grants were barely discernible in the distance.

Again threatening Abel with his revolver, Christian ordered him out of the cab and back to the express car. Here, they were joined by the other two bandits. Christian told Abel to unlock the door, but the fireman maintained he was not authorized to carry a key. Christian nodded to one of the outlaws who attached a dynamite charge to the heavy iron door. The four men ran for cover behind the trunk of a nearby cottonwood tree and seconds later the explosion tore apart the entire side of the express car. As Christian held the gun on Abel, the other two men entered the demolished car and located the heavy steel Wells Fargo safe. Another charge of dynamite was placed on the safe's door, and the subsequent explosion removed it and exploded the contents inside. When the smoke cleared, the outlaws dropped to their hands and knees and scooped up over $100,000 in gold and silver coins and placed them in saddlebags.

When the bags were filled, the two accomplices walked into the nearby woods, returning moments later with three horses that had been hidden there earlier. The outlaws mounted up. Just before they rode away into the night, Christian thanked Abel for being cooperative and bade him good night. Later, after Abel returned the train to the station, he told lawmen investigating the robbery that the outlaws rode away toward the south.

After reporting the robbery to the local authorities, Abel wired the Santa Fe offices and explained what happened. The railroad officials said they would send their detectives to the scene immediately. He then wired Wells Fargo and reported the theft of the safe's contents. The following afternoon, a posse composed of the Cibola County sheriff and some of his deputies, along with railroad detectives and Wells Fargo agents, departed Grants and headed toward the lava beds.

As the lawmen rode along, the sheriff explained to the agents and detectives that the lava beds, called *malpais* by the Mexicans, were a treacherous, rugged, and forbidding landscape composed of ancient, weathered basalt, the rock formed as a result of the cooling of a vast expanse of molten lava from eons-old volcanic eruptions in the region. The lava beds, he explained, were hundreds of feet thick in places, filled with deadly rattlesnakes and occasionally hostile Indians. The trails in the beds were narrow, deep, twisting, sinuous, and conducive to ambushes. Many men who entered the lava beds were never seen again.

Following the robbery of the Santa Fe train, Black Jack Christian and his partners rode hard all night, finally entering the lava beds and following a series of maze-like, narrow, zigzag trails, eventually arriving at an old Indian campsite deep inside the black expanse of rock. Here, they found a freshwater spring and enough grass for their tired mounts to graze. The high basalt walls offered protection from the consistent desiccating winds but, more importantly, afforded an excellent position from which the outlaws could defend themselves from approaching lawmen.

The following morning, after a meal of bacon cooked over a low campfire, the three outlaws decided it was time to relax a bit and celebrate their successful robbery. One of them pulled a bottle of whiskey from his saddlebags, opened it, and passed it around. For the next two hours as the morning sun rose and warmed the small enclosure within the basaltic rocks, the three men imbibed until they were drunk. Christian opened the saddlebags filled with the gold and silver coins and explained how the loot was to be divided. An argument about the split ensued immediately, and with the liquor fueling emotions, it soon became violent. One of Christian's henchman, angered by a comment by the other, pulled his revolver and shot his companion through the head, killing him instantly.

Several hours later when Christian and the surviving partner awoke from a whiskey-induced nap, they decided to bury their dead partner. With aching heads and queasy stomachs from their hangovers, the two had just completed the excavation of a shallow hole when they heard the sounds of riders in the distance. Christian climbed to an elevated knob where he could observe the trail without being seen. He spotted the posse less than one hundred yards away. Climbing down and hurrying back to the campsite, he told the other what he had seen and suggested it was time to make an escape before the lawmen stumbled onto their hiding place. Realizing the importance of haste and not wanting to be encumbered by the heavy saddlebags filled with coins as well as the canvas sack stuffed with jewelry, they tossed the loot into the hole. Atop the treasure, they placed the body of their dead companion. After quickly refilling the excavation, they saddled and mounted their horses and fled southward and out of the lava beds.

The posse, composed of fifteen men, entered the lava beds with optimism, convinced it was only a matter of time before they captured the outlaws. After three days of fruitless searching, however, they became disheartened, weary, and eager to return to Grants. Little had they realized that they passed within one hundred yards of the outlaws' campsite, and that Christian had watched them from his place of concealment. When they retuned to Grants, a large reward was offered for Black Jack Christian, dead or alive.

The next morning, after riding all night, Christian suggested that he and his partner separate and go their own ways to confuse any pursuing lawmen. They agreed to meet in thirty days at a tavern in Silver City, New Mexico. From there, Christian suggested, they would quietly return to the lava beds and retrieve the buried treasure.

Two weeks later, Black Jack Christian attempted another train robbery just a few miles from Silver City and was seriously wounded for his efforts. Bleeding profusely, he fell from his horse, was easily apprehended, and taken to Silver City where he was treated and charged with attempted robbery.

While Christian was fighting for his life in a Silver City clinic, his partner was attempting to rob yet another train in eastern Arizona. He was captured and sentenced to twenty years in the Territorial Prison at Yuma, but died from tuberculosis after serving only five years.

Black Jack Christian lived for only two days after his foiled robbery. Just before he died, he confessed to the Catron County sheriff his robbery of the Santa Fe train at Grants two weeks earlier, providing details of the crime and his escape. He described the killing of one partner by the other and the subsequent caching of the treasure. Prodded by the sheriff, Christian volunteered vague directions to the location. Weeks later, the sheriff led two expeditions into the lava beds in search of the buried train robbery loot. Once in the maze of basaltic rock, he found the outlaw's directions confusing and his estimated distances filled with error. Frustrated, he gave up, realizing that the only two men who knew the exact location of the buried railroad loot were dead.

During the month of July 1914, an out-of-work cowboy was traveling from Grants to Silver City in search of employment and attempted a short cut through the lava beds. Sundown found him entering a small grassy opening encircled by high black volcanic rock. There was sufficient grass for his horse, and at one end of the sward he found a freshwater spring. After filling his canteen, he built a small campfire and was boiling some coffee when he spotted a low mound of dirt not far from where he squatted. It resembled a grave, but he wasn't certain. Curious, he took a stick and dug into the mound. Just inches below the surface, he encountered a human skeleton and some rotted clothing. Unnerved by his discovery, he quickly refilled the hole and returned to his campfire.

Unknown to the itinerant cowboy, a fortune in gold and silver coins as well as money, jewelry, and watches reposed beneath the skeleton. Had he dug a little bit further, he would have been rewarded with a treasure that exceeded his wildest dreams and he would never have to face the rugged life of a cow hand again. Years later, when this cowboy was an old man with grandchildren, he learned the story of the robbery of the Santa Fe train by Black Jack Christian and the subsequent caching of the gold and silver coins and jewelry. The old cowboy realized he had accidentally stumbled upon the location during his trip through the lava beds decades earlier.

During the next two years, the old man undertook several trips into the rugged lava beds in an attempt to relocate the same little grassy campsite, the one with the freshwater spring and the low mound of dirt. He never found it.

Today, Black Jack Christian's train robbery loot is estimated to be worth well in excess of two million dollars. The lava beds where the treasure was cached are now the El Malpais National Monument. Those who have searched for this treasure have reported that there exist in this challenging landscape not one, but many such grassy, spring-fed environments. One of them, however, contains the skeleton of a train robber and a huge fortune only inches beneath the surface.

TIBURCIO VASQUEZ'S
500-POUND SILVER INGOT

During the early 1870s, newspapers throughout much of southern California were filled with stories of robberies and murder by the outlaw, Tiburcio Vasquez. Accompanied by a ruthless gang composed of murderers, thieves, and cutthroats, Vasquez preyed upon travelers and freight wagons going into and out of Los Angeles, often leaving his victims dead from bullet wounds or hanging by the neck from the nearest tree. Law enforcement authorities were constantly on the lookout for Vasquez and his gang and claimed to be patrolling the roads. The truth, however, was that the understaffed sheriff's departments in the many small towns were frightened of Vasquez, unprepared to deal with him, and preferred to stay as far away from the outlaw as possible.

One day in 1872, Vasquez and his band of outlaws robbed a freight wagon of a five-hundred-pound silver ingot. Within minutes after the robbery, the ingot was hidden among the rocks north of Los Angeles where it remains today.

William M. Stewart was a mining magnate who oversaw the extraction, processing, and sale of gold and silver throughout much of Nevada during that state's glory days. One of Stewart's important investments was the famous Comstock Lode from which he made millions. Stewart was not only a success in business and mining, but he also aspired to politics. To this new profession he brought the same energy, leadership abilities, and sense for organization as he did to mining, and he was eventually elected to the Nevada senate.

In 1872, Stewart traveled to southern California on a business trip. There, he met with his brother, and together the two men agreed to pool their resources and know-how and purchase a rich silver mine located in the mountains approximately 150 miles north of the city.

At least once about every six weeks, a shipment of silver ingots was sent from the mine to Los Angeles via mule train. While other miners and shippers in the area suffered depredations from Tiburcio Vasquez and his gang, the Stewart brothers' mining enterprise had never been bothered. One afternoon, however, as a pack train was being readied for a shipment, William Stewart received word that the outlaw was lying in wait along the trail to ambush the escort and take the silver.

Stewart immediately canceled plans for the shipment. He decided to delay transporting the silver for several days until Vasquez eventually grew tired of waiting and left the area. Three days later, Stewart's scouts informed him that Vasquez rode away from his place of concealment and traveled several miles to the east. There, he robbed another pack train, killed one of the guards, and retreated into their hideout in the mountains with his booty.

More time passed, and Stewart was informed of a plot by Vasquez to conduct a raid on the mine itself, taking whatever silver was processed into ingots and awaiting shipment. This information caused Stewart a great deal of worry, for he knew that his six Chinese laborers would be no match for Vasquez and his band of some twelve to twenty bandits.

Normally a calm and calculated man, Stewart grew frustrated with the knowledge of the impending attack. He had planned to sell the mine following this last shipment of silver to Los Angeles, and he feared that if the potential buyers learned of the depredations of Vasquez they might withdraw from the negotiation. Then, Stewart hit upon an idea that he was convinced would discourage the bandit.

Stewart's miners had approximately one thousand pounds of silver ingots packed and ready for shipment, dozens of small ingots that were to be placed into packs and loaded onto several mules. Stewart ordered his workers to construct two large ingot molds, re-melt the existing ingots, and pour the liquid into the new molds. Each of the resulting new ingots weighed just over five hundred pounds, and Stewart was convinced the great weight of the items would be enough to discourage their theft.

Around midmorning of the following day, an informant rode to the mine and warned Stewart that Vasquez and his men were planning to strike early the next day, take all the silver they could pack onto two mules, and then ride away to San Francisco where they hoped to sell it at a good price and where there were no lawmen looking for them.

Around dawn on the day of the anticipated raid, Stewart left the two five-hundred-pound ingots lying on the floor of the building where they were formed. He sent his men away and, grabbing a pair of binoculars, climbed to the top of a nearby hill where he concealed himself among some rock and brush and awaited the arrival of the bandits.

Around two hours past sunrise, two Mexicans on horseback rode up to the wooden frame headquarters building, each leading a mule. As he watched intently through binoculars, Stewart recognized the riders as two men he had beaten badly at cards several weeks earlier in a Los Angeles tavern. The two men were known to ride with the Vasquez gang from time to time. Finding the headquarters building vacant, the two outlaws explored around the buildings, trying to act casual. Eventually, they entered the large building where the two ingots lay on the floor.

From his vantage point high on the nearby hill, Stewart could hear the cursing of the two Mexicans as they tried to move the silver. Gathering some nearby materials, they proceeded to construct a tripod with a pulley and a sling just outside the building. With great difficulty, they dragged one of the ingots out of the building and under the structure. As they attempted to raise the object, one of the legs of the tripod snapped and it toppled over.

After another half-hour, the two men succeeded in building another tripod. When they raised the heavy ingot this time, this tripod, like the first one, broke and collapsed to the ground. On the third attempt, the ingot was finally raised high enough such that one of the mules could be led to a position beneath it. When they attempted to lower the ingot into a crate strapped to the back of one of the mules, the rope broke. The great weight of the ingot struck the mule, startling it. The frightened animal bolted away and up the hill, passing only a few feet from where Stewart crouched in hiding.

By midafternoon, Stewart grew tired of observing what he regarded as the foolish attempts of the two outlaws and took a nap. Presently, the Mexicans gave up and rode away, leaving the two ingots behind. Stewart climbed down the hill and returned to the headquarters. Convinced Vasquez and his gang would not make a second attempt on the silver, he began to make preparations to ship the two ingots to Los Angeles the next morning.

Stewart contracted the services of a successful freighter named Remi Nadeau. Nadeau possessed a fleet of wagons and a stock of well-bred draft horses. Stewart had done business with Nadeau before and had been pleased with the results. Nadeau was well-respected throughout the southern California region and shippers could count on their deliveries arriving safely at the designated destination. Nadeau also employed a contingent of armed guards to accompany valuable shipments such as ore.

There was yet another reason why Stewart wanted Nadeau to transport his silver ingots into Los Angeles. The outlaw Tiburcio Vasquez was never known to rob a Nadeau shipment. Stewart never knew the reason the bandit stayed away from Nadeau wagons, but it was learned many years later that Remi Nadeau, while transporting some freight one day, came upon a wounded and almost dead Vasquez lying in the dust of the road. A few hours earlier, Vasquez had attempted to rob another freight wagon and was shot several times and left bleeding on the ground. Nadeau loaded the unconscious Vasquez into his wagon and carried him to his freight station where he nursed him back to health. Since then, a Nadeau-owned freight wagon had never been molested by the bandit. At least, not until the day Stewart decided to have Nadeau ship his two silver ingots.

Two days later, the heavy ingots were loaded onto the back of a stout wagon. The driver, a man named James Funk, was accompanied by four armed guards. From the mine, the ingots were hauled to the town of Panamint where they were transferred to another wagon, a larger one carrying other freight bound for Los Angeles. When the transfer was completed, Funk steered the wagon out onto the road, flanked front and rear and side to side by the armed, mounted guards.

Approaching Los Angeles from the north, Funk guided the wagon along the winding road that snaked through an area known today as the Vasquez Hills. The region was characterized by hundreds of exposed granite outcrops and boulders distributed across more than a thousand acres. A number of these outcrops were in excess of two hundred feet tall, were highly weathered, and contained thousands of shallow pits eroded out of the igneous mass. The natural pits, some of them three to four feet deep, often contained water following a rain, and were called *tinajas* by the Mexicans.

When Funk and his escort were about halfway through the maze of boulders, they were attacked. The guards, taken completely by surprise, threw down their guns and surrendered. Tiburcio Vasquez himself rode up to Funk, ordered him off of the wagon at gunpoint, then dismounted and climbed into the driver's seat. Vasquez drove the buckboard some distance away from the scene and into the nearby rocks. Here, with the help of two of his henchmen, he slid one of the ingots from the wagon bed. With difficulty, the three men carried the heavy object to one of the *tinajas* and dropped it within.

When the task was completed, Vasquez rode back to the scene of the attack. He freed Funk and the guards, sending them on to Los Angeles unharmed. On arriving in the city, Funk reported the robbery to the sheriff, then notified his employer, Nadeau. Within the hour, the sheriff gathered a posse and rode out toward the Vasquez Hills, his objective to encounter the outlaw and his gang and kill or capture them.

When they finally arrived at the place where the wagon had been stopped, the posse conducted a search throughout the boulder-strewn area. About two hours later, they found the abandoned wagon with the horses still hitched to it. Inside the wagon were the goods destined for Los Angeles and the remaining silver ingot. Though the sheriff and his men searched the region for the rest of the day, they were unable to find the other ingot. The sheriff deduced Vasquez must have somehow escaped with it.

A month later, Tiburcio Vasquez and his band were at work once again. This time, the outlaw tried to extort $800 from a rancher named Repetto. Repetto, who was in his seventies, owned a large ranch just outside of the Los Angeles city limits. A few hours after Vasquez departed the Repetto ranch, the old man notified the sheriff who once again organized a posse and gave chase. This time, the lawmen caught up with Vasquez and his gang near a location that is now Hollywood. Following a brief gun battle, Vasquez, who had been struck several times, was taken prisoner. After his wounds were treated and bandaged, he was transported to San Jose where he was charged with at least half a dozen offenses. A few weeks later he was tried, convicted of the murder of two passengers during an earlier stagecoach robbery, and sentenced to hang.

Several days after his conviction, Vasquez was visited in his cell by his old friend Nadeau. The freighter asked the bandit why, after all the years of avoiding his freight wagons, he decided to rob the one containing the silver ingots. Vasquez apologized and told Nadeau he needed the money badly and reminded him that he took only one of the two ingots.

Nadeau asked the outlaw what he did with the ingot, and Vasquez told him he dropped it into one of the *tinajas* in the rocks not far from where he stopped the freight wagon.

On several occasions, both Nadeau and Stewart visited the Vasquez Hills to look for the five-hundred-pound silver ingot, but to no avail. Both men, along with those they employed to help them with the search, were surprised to find hundreds of such holes.

To this day, the silver ingot has never been found, and undoubtedly it still lies at the bottom of one of the many *tinajas* found in these hills.

It is common for these shallow pits to become partially or entirely filled in with sediment, either from sand and dust blowing in from storms, or from the natural weathering and accumulation of the old and crumbling granite. As a result, an object such as a large silver ingot could easily have been covered up over the years. With patience, some luck, and a high-quality metal detector, some fortunate treasure hunter may stumble upon this valuable object some day, and when he does, he will be richer by a quarter of a million dollars.

THE LOST IRON DOOR TREASURE
OF THE OUTLAW BELLE STARR

One of American history's strangest tales of lost treasure involves the outlaw Belle Starr. By most standards, Starr was a small-time criminal, and though colorful, was mostly known for providing sanctuary at her home in eastern Oklahoma to more famous outlaws such as the James brothers and the Younger brothers. It is also believed by many that Starr helped her outlaw friends plan crimes and aided them in both hiding and spending the money and gold taken in bank and train robberies.

The story of Belle Starr, like most outlaw figures in American history, has taken on the elements of legend which, as time passes, becomes difficult to distinguish from fact. Much of Starr's life has been documented and told in books and articles. Less is known about her mysterious cache located somewhere in the Wichita Mountains of southwestern Oklahoma, a trove of U.S. government gold reportedly worth more than half a million dollars.

Sometime during the 1880s, legend relates that Starr and her gang stopped a freight train bound for the Denver Mint. The train was transporting a cargo of gold ingots destined to be turned into coin. Though the robbery went smoothly, the gang feared immediate pursuit from federal agents, so they decided to cache the loot until things cooled down. They selected a cave in the Wichita Mountains that was known to them. Just prior to riding away from the site of the robbery, gang members removed a large iron door from one of the railroad cars, and using ropes, dragged it along behind as they made their escape on horseback. Once the gold had been stacked against one wall of the cave, the iron door was placed over the entrance, wedged into position with heavy rocks and mortar, secured with an intricate lock, and covered over with more rock and brush. Before leaving the area, it was said that one of the outlaws hammered a railroad spike into an oak tree about one hundred yards from the cave.

During a subsequent train robbery attempt a few months later, all of the gang members save for Starr were killed. In 1889, Belle Starr was mysteriously murdered, a crime that has never been solved. With her death, no one remained alive who knew the exact location of what has come to be known as "The Iron Door Cache."

Railroad detectives eventually learned of the possibility that the stolen gold had been cached in the Wichitas and, though they searched for weeks, could never find it. With the passage of years, however, the matter was eventually forgotten.

During the first decade of the twentieth century, a rancher and his son were riding through a portion of the Wichita Mountains toward the home of some friends who lived in the small town of Indiahoma, located on the south side of the range. After getting a late start and afraid they might not arrive at their destination before nightfall, they took a little-known shortcut through an unfamiliar part of the mountains. The trail, they recalled later, skirted Elk Mountain and entered a deep canyon. As they rode along, their attention was captured by the sharp reflection of the setting sun from an object located on the east wall of the canyon. On investigating, they came upon a large, rusted, iron door set into a recessed area part of the canyon wall. The door was partially covered with rock and debris. They wanted to examine the site further, to see what might lie beyond the odd door, but the father, determined to reach their friend's house before nightfall, insisted they leave. He promised the boy they would return soon to see what was behind the door.

Later that evening when they arrived at their destination, the father described the iron door they found in the canyon and asked if anyone else had ever seen it. Their host grew quite excited at this news and related the tale of Belle Starr's train robbery and the subsequent caching of the stolen gold shipment.

Early the next morning, the father, son, and the host retraced the path taken the evening before. After entering the canyon, they searched along the east wall but were unable to find the iron door. The host suggested it might not be the right canyon, so they searched another, then another, but still failed to locate the door. During the next ten years, the father and son searched the area several more times, exploring several canyons in this part of the range, but their quest to catch a glimpse of the iron door remained unfulfilled. They determined that it was important to be at a certain location in the canyon during a particular moment of sunset in order to catch the sun's rays striking the metal object, but they never found themselves in the right canyon at the right time.

In 1908, an elderly woman who gave her name only as Holt arrived in the Wichita Mountains by wagon. She stated she had traveled alone all the way from Missouri and had in her possession a map that allegedly showed the location of the iron door cache. She also carried a large key which, she said, was supposed to unlock the door. When interviewed, she told how she came into possession of the map and key.

The old woman said that years earlier she treated the wounds of a dying outlaw who claimed to have been a member of the gang that rode with Belle Starr, robbed the gold from the train, cached it in a cave in the Wichita Mountains, and covered the opening with an iron boxcar door. Before the outlaw died, he sketched a crude map showing the location of the cave and gave her a key that he said would unlock the large iron door that covered the entrance. He also told her that not far from the cache was a large oak tree into which had been hammered a railroad spike.

In 1910, a group of teenagers was exploring a remote canyon in the Wichita Mountains when they encountered the iron door. Later, one of the boys provided a description of the door and the large, rusted padlock that held it shut. The boys assumed the cave behind the door was being used by some local rancher to store feed and supplies, so they left it alone. After the passage of several years, one of the boys learned the story of Belle Starr's iron door cache. Now a grown man with a family, he determined to return to the canyon and relocate it. He traveled many times to what he thought was the same canyon, but repeatedly failed to find the iron door. He was convinced the canyon was located just north of Treasure Lake, the same general area identified by the father and son many years earlier.

During the 1920s, a group of men was hunting raccoons in a remote canyon of the Wichita Mountains. Early one evening, one of their dogs treed a raccoon and a hunter hurried to get a shot at the animal. Just as he was taking aim, he was distracted by a sharp reflection from the opposite wall of the canyon. Curious, he climbed atop a nearby boulder to get a better look at the source of the glare and saw that it was coming from what he believed was a large iron door set into a recessed portion of the canyon wall. As it was late and the hunters had a long way to go to reach their camp, they left, determined to return another day and investigate the piece of iron.

Six weeks later, the hunters returned to what they believed was the same location but were unable to locate the iron door. Like others who encountered the iron door, they stated that it was in a canyon not far from Treasure Lake.

Around 1930, three boys were walking through the Wichita Mountains to Indiahoma. In a hurry, they decided to take a shortcut through a canyon they were convinced would save them some time. As they described it later, the hike through this canyon took them past a large, rusty iron door set into the side of the mountain. The boys climbed up to the strange door and examined it and the large padlock that held it secure. Unaware of the huge fortune in gold ingots that lay just beyond the iron door, the boys hiked on. In 1981, one of them, now a rancher, learned the story of Belle Starr's iron door gold cache from a local Indian. Convinced it was the same door he had seen five decades earlier as a boy, the rancher tried to relocate the canyon. Like the others who have searched for the iron door, he failed. All he could remember from the early trip with his friends was that the door was found in a canyon near Treasure Lake.

In 1932, a migrant farm worker was walking from Hobart, Oklahoma, to Lawton in search of work. His journey took him through the Wichita Mountains. One evening, he made a crude camp, prepared a poor meal of beans and coffee, and fell asleep. The next morning, he continued on his trek and followed a path that took him through a canyon near Elk Mountain. As he passed through the canyon, he saw a "rust-stained door . . . barely exposed on the mountainside." The farm worker knew the story of the lost iron door treasure cache and was certain he had found it. He climbed up the slope to the door and strained for nearly an hour trying to get it open. He removed dozens of large rocks from in front of it and uprooted and cleared away a great deal of brush. He finally determined it would take some heavy tools to break the lock and wedge the huge door from its position in the cave entrance. Three days later in Lawton, he enlisted the help of two men who supplied the necessary tools, along with some dynamite. When the three men returned to the canyon identified by the farm worker, the door could not be found. They searched for a full day, covering the same trail many times, but were unable to relocate the iron door.

During the 1940s, a man named Stephens reported he found the iron door. Aware of the story of the lost cache, he immediately recognized it for what it was. Stephens said he was hiking in a canyon not far from Treasure Lake when he spotted it recessed into one wall not far from the trail and partially concealed with rocks and brush. He described the door as being one associated with very old railroad cars. He tried to pry the huge door open but was unsuccessful. He decided to travel back to his home and return with the tools necessary to remove the door and gain access to the treasure beyond. Just before he left the area, he constructed a cairn of rocks at a nearby trail crossing to help him relocate the canyon on his return trip. When Stephens returned several weeks later with tools and a group of men, he could locate neither the cairn nor the canyon.

During the 1950s, a rancher was riding through an unnamed canyon in the Wichita Mountains during the middle of a summer day when he spotted a large oak tree and decided to take shade under it for a while, resting himself and his horse. While his horse grazed on some nearby grasses, the rancher hung his hat on an old railroad spike that had long ago been hammered into the trunk, lay down, and slept for an hour. Like others who experienced a close encounter with the iron door cache, the rancher heard the story of the robbery and the hiding of the gold several years later, along with an allusion to the oak tree with the railroad spike in it. He made several attempts to relocate the canyon but was unsuccessful. He later learned that someone cut down the tree for firewood.

Some day some fortunate treasure hunter will find himself in the right canyon just as the setting sun is reflecting off of the iron door set into the mountainside. With luck, the searcher may be able to return to the location with the equipment necessary to pry the door from its setting and recover the fortune in gold ingots lying just inside the cave.

MULTIMILLION DOLLAR GANGSTER TREASURE

It has been estimated that hundreds of millions of dollars in cash, bonds, gold, and jewelry reaped by organized crime during the 1920s and 1930s was hidden, secreted away in a variety of locations around the country in order to keep it from the prying eyes of law enforcement agents, the Internal Revenue Service, and curious bookkeepers employed by the nation's banks. In many instances, the treasure was never recovered, for those who were responsible for caching it were either killed or sentenced to prison for life. Now and then, however, some of this wealth is found, but the majority of it remains lost. One of the most provocative tales of lost treasure from organized crime is associated with the gangster Dutch Schultz, and the hoard, if found, would be worth more than $100 million today.

During the 1920s, one of organized crime's most powerful and effective mobsters was a man named Arthur Flegenheimer who went by the nickname Dutch Schultz. By 1922, Schultz, still a very young man, had risen to a prominent position in the world of organized crime and operated a number of rackets including illegal taverns, gambling houses, distilleries, bootlegging, nightclubs, houses of prostitution, and others. Federal agents regarded Schultz as a major kingpin and worked overtime to try to break up his criminal enterprises. It has been estimated Schultz pocketed over twenty million dollars during the first few years of the 1920s alone. As Schultz attained a position of power among the country's most prominent criminals, he hired a man named Bernard "Lulu" Rosencranz as his aide, driver, and bodyguard.

By 1932, Schultz was regarded as one of the most powerful criminals in the United States. Federal law enforcement officials named him Public Enemy Number One and redoubled their effort to take him down. Though agents arrested Schultz many times on charges of robbery, murder, violation of prohibition laws, and dozens of other crimes, he always managed to evade prosecution. Schultz proudly and arrogantly boasted he had spent millions of dollars in payoffs to government officials to keep from going to prison.

Though sought for committing numerous violent crimes and regarded as one of the nation's most dangerous men, Schultz was eventually charged with income tax evasion. When he was informed of his impending arrest, Schultz fled to Bridgeport, Connecticut, under cover of night where he gathered up $150 million of his accumulated wealth in cash, bonds, and diamonds along with other precious stones and gold coins. After placing the fortune in a specially made iron chest, Schultz, with the help of Rosencranz, drove away from Bridgeport in the gangster's bullet-proof Packard and traveled to the small New York town of Phoenicia, located twenty-two miles northwest of Kingston on State Highway 28. After arriving in Phoenicia, Schultz ordered Rosencranz to drive a short distance out of town to the banks of Esopus Creek. Here, Rosencranz was instructed to dig a two-and-a-half-foot-deep hole in the forest of pines and sycamores. This done, the aide dragged the heavy chest from the Packard and placed it in the hole, then refilled the excavation. Following this, Schultz swore Rosencranz to secrecy and sent him away. Several weeks later, Schultz, tiring of running and hiding from the tightening pursuit of lawmen, finally surrendered to authorities in Albany, New York.

Though he was not wanted by the law, Lulu Rosencranz remained in hiding, rarely surfacing except to fraternize occasionally with other criminals. Lulu's best friend was a small-time thief named Marty Krompier, and the two men often met for drinks at a Brooklyn tavern. After one evening of heavy drinking, Lulu told Marty about the chest filled with Dutch Schultz's treasure buried near the bank of the Esopus River outside of Phoenicia. Taking advantage of Lulu's state of inebriation, Krompier encouraged his friend to reveal all of the details he could remember about the location and the contents of the chest. He also convinced Lulu to sketch a map showing the location of the wealthy cache. With the map in his possession, Krompier began making plans to travel to Phoenicia and dig up the treasure for himself should Schultz be sent to prison for a long time.

Gangster Schultz, after paying off a number of law enforcement agents, prosecutors, and, some say, a judge as well as members of the jury, was acquitted. Shortly after the acquittal, Schultz moved to Newark, New Jersey, where he rented a room above the Palace Chop House and

Tavern. Within weeks, he was back to his criminal ways and, it is said, was soon responsible for dozens of murders.

Thomas E. Dewey, the chief assistant to the United States attorney for the southern district of New York and the future governor of the state, specialized in investigating organized crime. Dewey decided it was time to apply more pressure to Dutch Schultz and his gang, and he ordered that the gangster be followed twenty-four hours a day. Schultz retaliated by planning an assassination of Dewey, but erred grievously when he went around town bragging about his plan.

Several of Schultz's companions were annoyed by the talk of killing Dewey. If such a thing happened, they insisted, efforts to get rid of organized crime in New York would increase, making it more difficult for them to carry on their illegal activities. They pleaded for Dewey to abandon the idea, but the gangster ignored them.

Arrogant with power, Schultz began moving his operations into the territories of some of his contemporaries, taking over their activities. Angered, his newfound enemies, who were already miffed at his plans to assassinate Dewey, held a secret meeting and decided to have Schultz eliminated. They sent a pair of professional killers to do the job.

On October 24, 1941, the two hit men encountered Lulu Rosencranz and inquired about the whereabouts of Schultz. Rosencranz was unable to provide any information and was shot down. As an ambulance carried the mortally wounded man to the hospital, the assassins continued their search for Shultz. Less than an hour later they found him, and with no preliminaries, they filled the crime kingpin with bullets.

At the moment Schultz was being gunned down, Lulu Rosencranz lay dying in a hospital room in New York City. He knew he would not live much longer, and before he died, he called a young nurse to his side and told her the story of Dutch Schultz's buried treasure near the bank of Esopus Creek. He asked her to fetch a pencil and a piece of paper so he could draw her a map, but before she returned he had died.

At the same time, Schultz hovered near death in a Newark hospital. When he was told of Rosencranz's death, he sagged into his bed and expressed sadness at the loss of his friend. Next to Schultz's bedside sat John Long, a police stenographer who had been instructed to write down any information the dying gangster might volunteer relative to his long string of robberies and murders. Investigators were also curious as to what had become of Schultz's wealth.

Following a few minutes of questioning, Schultz told of transporting $150 million in gold, bank notes, bonds, and diamonds to a remote location near the town of Phoenicia where it was buried. Schultz provided only vague directions. A few hours later, he died.

Using the information provided by Schultz, investigators traveled to Phoenicia the following day and attempted to locate the place where the treasure was buried, but the directions provided by the dying gangster proved meaningless.

With the death of Schultz, only two people remained alive who possessed details regarding his buried treasure: Krompier, and the nurse who attended Rosencranz. Krompier decided that, with Schultz and Rosencranz gone, it was time to retrieve the fortune from its hiding place and become a wealthy man.

While packing for his trip to Phoenicia, however, Krompier discovered he had lost the map provided by Lulu. After searching through his belongings several times, he decided to proceed without it, believing he could remember the directions well enough to retrieve the treasure.

On arriving in Phoenicia, Krompier became confused as to which road to follow. He drove out of the town along two or three different routes but became lost each time. He failed to locate any landmarks he recalled from Lulu's descriptions. Dejected, he gave up and returned home.

After Krompier had been home for about a week, he found the map. Excited, he placed it in his wallet and made plans to return to Phoenicia to locate the chest filled with treasure. Unfortunately for him, he bragged about his good luck that evening in a local tavern.

The next day, Marty Krompier was shot and killed in a barber chair while getting a haircut. His killer was Jake Shapiro, a rival hoodlum. After shooting him, Shapiro grabbed Krompier's wallet, removed the map, and fled from the scene.

Now in possession of the treasure map, Shapiro decided to travel to Phoenicia and dig up Schultz's treasure. When he arrived in the small town, however, he was unable to decipher the map or comprehend the directions. He searched for two days with no success and decided to return home. Two days later, Shapiro was arrested in Kingston, New York, and charged with the murder of Marty Krompier. He was tried, convicted, and sentenced to death. Months later he was executed in the electric chair at Sing Sing Prison. When Shapiro was arrested, he was not in possession of the map taken from Krompier's wallet, and what became of it has never been learned.

Several years following the death of Rosencranz, the nurse came forward with the set of directions he provided. She employed a pair of fortune hunters to locate the treasure for her but they never found it.

The location of Dutch Schultz's treasure, worth $150 million in the 1920s, has been assigned a value in excess of one billion dollars today. It still lies in the ground somewhere near Esopus Creek just outside of Phoenicia, New York.